NAKED
GRACE

A Quest For Clarity
In A World Of Confusion

Lucas Kitchen

Published in association with
Free Grace International
WWW.FREEGRACE.IN

OTHER BOOKS BY
LUCAS KITCHEN:

Christian Non-Fiction
Eternal Life: Believe To Be Alive
Salvation and Discipleship: Is There A Difference?
Eternal Rewards: It Will Pay To Obey
Thomas: Hero Of The Faith
Questions From Atheists

Christian Children's Books:
Good Enough
Evan Wants To Go To Heaven
Adventures In Mudville

Novels:
Infinite Tomorrow
Cloud Haven
Below The Huber Ice
World Builder
Divine Children

Dedicated to Kristah.
You rescued me from my meaningless meandering.

TABLE OF CONTENTS

DISCLAIMER

Being that this is a true story, the names in this book have been changed to protect the innocent. Well, I guess no one is innocent. Actually, the names have been changed to make sure I don't get sued. As far as I remember, the rest is true, except for the parts I made up.

EMOTIONS

If your parents didn't take you to an amusement park as a kid, they either didn't love you or…. No, that's pretty much it, they didn't love you. The park of choice for those near Dallas is the famed Six Flags over Texas. It's a theme park with towering roller coasters, fair-style games, a steam train, and all of the excitement you'd expect from a Texas-sized tourist attraction. It's daily jammed with hoards of people looking for adventure and escape from the mundane. As a kid, I had no defense against its magical allure.

The year was 1988. Precisely 71.4% of my childhood was spent thinking about my next chance to enter the gates of Six Flags. My mind buzzed with the electric anticipation as we approached the colorful arches adorning the entrance. Holiday in the Park, as they called it, included all of the summer attractions with one added bonus, fake snow.

Along with my parents, my nuclear family unit included my little brother Levi who could clearly express himself even at a young age, and never backed down from a challenge to do so. He and I shared a familiar humor, often squeezing endless laughter out of the most bizarre corners of life.

My older brother Lance always had his eyes on the horizon, looking for our next quest. If there was a blunt force concussion available, Lance would claim it. He was a quiet leader, expressing his feelings often without the use of words.

Six Flags was a treat for all three of us. Mom stuffed my six-year-old body into a blue vinyl hand-me-down coat. It, too, was Lance's first. As we darted through the front gate, the first ride that greeted these intrepid amusement seekers was a massive carousel. It was a holdover from the early days of the park before roller coasters were a standard affair. Lance was the benevolent dictator of our little gang—hardly a wolf pack—pups at best. His eyes locked on the ride with crackling enthusiasm.

"Can we ride that one?" Lance asked, as if his life depended on it.

"Of course, Honey," Mom said. The spark in his eyes lit a fire in Levi, although the youngest was hardly old enough to know what thrill he was about to experience.

Mom and Dad helped us up the stairs. Lance chose the blue plastic steed for its masculine appeal. "I can get on myself," he reprimanded those who would help.

Levi and I followed, accepting what help Mom and Dad provided.

"Here we go," Dad said as the carousel whirred to life. The lights danced, and the stallions began to gallop in slow, methodical rhythm. Mom and Dad watched with that warm satisfaction that bubbles up from somewhere deep when a child smiles.

Lance's horse wasn't fast enough, so he made up for his mount's lackadaisical gait with a repetitive bounce. The plastic saddle creaked as he jumped and shouted with delight. There was no question; he was having the time of his young life. Levi's response was much the same. Although smaller, he gripped the pole with the experienced little hands of a thrill seeker. His curly hair danced in the chilling breeze. The look on his face spoke of the volcanic excitement that was erupting within.

"What's wrong with Lucas?" Dad asked, pointing to me. They both glanced in my direction. My riding style was a far cry from the wild abandon my brothers were experiencing. My gaze was measured; my grip was firm; my face was emotionless. "Is he not having fun?" Dad questioned.

Unlike my brothers, I was not comfortable with exuberant expressions of emotion. I preferred a calculated response. Any expectation to the contrary would drive me deeper into the emotional hermit house where I lived. I had feelings, but they would dissolve in the sunlight, so I hid them in the dark shadows of my dusty cabin.

"He's having a great time," Mom said. "He just doesn't show it." Mom had long since noted the differences in her three boys. I avoided putting my own emotions on display. My feelings were like a losing hand of cards, and I had a master poker face.

My lack of ability to express my feelings resulted in some surprising gullibilities. In the following year or so, I recall standing in the front yard with my brother Lance. We were throwing the baseball back and forth. He was experimenting with a new way to throw the ball, always the innovator. He awkwardly thrust it with a movement that might be used by a shot-putter who is being attacked by killer bees. The ball met the ground far short of its target. The experiment had been a failure.

"That's how they throw the ball in Asia," Lance said with utter conviction. Any normal kid would have expressed confusion, disbelief, or amazement. I was no ordinary kid. I quietly considered the new information I had just received. Rather than question my brother's audacious international claim, I wondered how an entire continent could be so dumb as not to know how to throw a baseball properly. I believed this ridiculous claim for years, never questioning its validity. That is until I caught a snippet of a World Series game between the A-list American team, and Japan's finest. Those Japanese kids rocketed the ball just like I'd seen in the American major leagues. I realized at that moment, after years of confusion, that Lance had been joking.

One summer day I was leaning against the screen door of our house. I was in the throes of indecision, trying to determine whether I wanted to play outside or in. I leaned my face against the screen letting my nose rest against its fine mesh.

"That screen will melt your nose off," Lance said as he sped by on his way outside. I pulled back with a shock. I wondered if there was some acidic property inherent in all screens, or if he was referring to the cheese grater effect. Either way, I was pretty fond of my nose, so I stopped pressing my face against the screen door.

A kid with a more developed emotional range might express confusion, misunderstanding, or disbelief. Not me. It made more sense to believe my older brother. Though, here's where it gets weird. For years I was cautious when touching any screen, whether it be on a window or door. Bouncing around in my subconscious was the idea that, 'screens can melt your nose off.' At some point it occurred to me from where my trepidation had come. I lived with the confusion for years, but eventually put the idea in my mental wastebasket.

"She has a disease that makes it where she can't smile or laugh," he once said about one of our church's piano players. It was a plausible explanation for what I had observed. It explained well the solemn and serious woman's perpetual sad state. I had never heard of such a disease, but rather than question my brother's accuracy I decidedly lived in a state of misinformation. It wasn't until years later when I saw the woman laugh out loud that I realized I had once again taken a joke as a fact.

Throughout my life, I've often assumed people who speak with conviction are right and truthful. Often when what I heard did not fit with what I already knew, I assumed the error was mine, not the speaker's. What further exacerbated the problem is my lack of willingness to express my feelings in these confusing situations. I am the emotional chameleon always playing along never admitting confusion, shock, or disbelief. I internalize and consider rarely ever admitting I don't understand.

This book is about the journey of a confused kid seeking to understand the most crucial topic.

BUNK BED TEARS

A father's nightly rituals are a thing of boundless fascination to his son. His endless hours at work might as well have been spent in a mysterious patch of the Brazilian Amazon as in an office building two miles from the house. My brothers and I would anticipate the nightly ambush we planned to lay on our unsuspecting father. At the moment of his triumphal return there was a mandatory wrestling match in which I would make dark-hearted threats like, "I'm going to squeeze your hand too hard." That's right; that was my attempt at the blackest of intimidations. We would reenact all of the karate kicks we'd learned from the day's TV binge-fest. Each night the mock battle raged between Father and sons. We spilled much imaginary blood on that shaggy orange living room carpet.

The fathers of a lot of my friends drank a beer in the

evenings, if not a few. I remember the first time I visited a neighborhood friend and spotted the icy cans of Miller in the refrigerator. His father's billiard room with a massive beer fridge, was the centerpiece of the house. An uneasy feeling came over me as I stared into the cooler containing the unfamiliar brew. His beer-drinking dad was a great guy. He took the family to Catholic Mass weekly, played football in the yard, and cracked open a cold one every night. Beer was just a part of their lives. It wasn't part of ours.

My dad's routine never included alcohol. He had enjoyed occasional drinking before he had kids, but he gave it up for his child-raising years. Once, however, I saw him sipping champagne at the wedding reception of one of his life-long friends. He let me try some knowing it would result in a crinkled nose and gut-level revulsion. Though raising three boys had to be like a twenty-pound sledgehammer to the chin, he handled it as a man should. He didn't lean on a cold beverage to drive away the edgy stress of the day, managing the ups and downs of being a college professor and freelance illustrator without anything but positivity and a sunny disposition to aid his ever bright mood.

As the sun crept low and the calls for bedtime began to ring from Mom's evening reading nook, Dad could often be found in his recliner trying to stave off the drowsiness the day's tasks had wrought. He wasn't picky about programming. He would watch whatever the cheapest cable-TV package offered. The creak of his second-hand rocking chair, the plaid pattern of its out of style and well-worn material, and the rests rubbed smooth and shiny from years of forearm friction is where he found his end-of-day relaxation.

In those sleepy after work hours, he could have insisted on alone-time, or man-time, or shut-your-mouths-you-little-brats-time, but he wasn't selfish. From his three wild and often barefoot boys, he didn't demand anything that wasn't reasonable for a child to give. He offered consistency in his temperament and the kind of predictability a kid wants from an authority figure three times their size. His discipline was measured, calm, and strategic. He hugged after every spanking and spoke in a controlled tone at every correction.

There was one thing that my father did every night without exception. After each of us had crawled below the covers and nestled in for the nocturnal hours, Dad would get up from his chair, no matter how tired he was. He would quietly enter the bedroom of his three boys. He would sit on the edge of the bed and do something that was like treasure to an adoring son. He would talk for a few minutes with each. In those dusky moments he taught us how to do what men the world over do. He didn't lecture, prattle, or blubber, but instead showed his eager kids how much fun it is to have a conversation, a discussion, a meaningful talk. At the end of the bedside chat, we would pray together before he sent us off worry-free to the land of dewy dreams.

Through constancy and commitment to his three little men, he built a trust like Gibraltar that was near unshakable. It doesn't seem fair. Plenty of kids throughout my hometown went to bed after being yelled at by a scary red-faced man whom their mom refused to break up with. At those same soul-crushing moments, while other children's little hearts were turned to coal by fear, I basked in the glory that a good dad brings to a household. I spent the last few moments of every night chatting and praying with a man I knew loved me, a man who would kick the teeth out of anyone who tried to harm me.

Through prayer and conversation he opened the doors to the minds of three boys who would soon be asking the big questions. He knew that someone would answer those questions and he wanted to be the one sitting there, in the dark, when those questions came. One day in late October, Dad's firstborn, my trailblazing brother, asked one of the biggies with the kind of gusto befitting the oldest.

"Why are you crying?" Dad asked Lance, who had the coveted top bunk.

"Dad, are we going to run out of air?" Lance gulped, fighting back sobs.

"No, Buddy. Of course not. Why do you ask that?"

Dad said as he wiped away his tears.

"You remember the movie we watched, Robinson Crusoe On Mars? He ran out of air." Lance said.

That was it. That was all the opening Dad needed to give reassurance to his frightened son, both for this life and the next. Dad used it as an opportunity to talk to Lance about the free gift of salvation. After reassuring him that our atmospheric pressure wasn't going to fail anytime soon, Dad spelled out the basics of the gospel so that a seven-year-old might understand. After explaining in slow deliberate words, Dad prayed with Lance as they always did. There would be more conversations to come, but something beautiful had begun.

I had been eavesdropping from my shadowy bunk below. There are no secrets among bunk bed brothers. When my father knelt to sit at the corner of my bed, he was surprised to find that I was crying as well. That was not an occurrence all that uncommon. I was often found wetly weeping in the first decade of my life. He began to question me, trying to discover what had broken the fragile wits of his emotionally frail middle son.

"I want to be saved too," I said, fearing that I would be left out. Like a kid whose brother just got an ice cream cone, I was moved to righteous jealousy. I didn't know what he was talking about on the top bunk, but I wanted in. That is the ever-present curse of being the second born. It took longer than usual to return Dad to his recliner that night. My thoughts were too smeared by tears to grasp the significance at that moment. Some mustard seeds were planted in the soft soil of our hearts. The conversation continued for a few days.

THE DRAWING TABLE

Not many days after the bunk bed incident, I was standing by my Dad's drawing table. The walls of his studio were always crowded with drying paintings. That's where he would work when he had freelance illustration jobs. At that time, he was building upon a budding career as a painter for hire. From children's books to massive outdoor murals, his projects always sparked our imaginations and inspired our creativity. We'd intently watch as he'd pucker his lips and brush out tight practiced lines. The brothers and I would often imitate, sprawling out underfoot crayons in hand, creating our masterpieces. He would lean down, giving appropriate praise for our works of art. Though no praise was void of the instruction of a master art teacher.

This night was different. On the green vinyl of his

drawing table, he placed and opened a family Bible that was at least as large as my head. My little brother once bragged that his head was the size of the kitchen cabinet. We're a big-headed people. The Bible was head-big. As he flipped, the spine cracked and glossy biblical scenes fanned before my eyes. I was mesmerized by Moses, wild-haired, standing before the Red Sea; Abraham with stone knife raised high above his son Issac, and Jonah being puked from the mouth of a large fish. What strange mysteries this book held. I marveled at the enigmatic allure, the magic of what was printed in those pages. The Bible finally fell open to the Gospel of John, chapter three. His thick finger pointed out the paragraph then grazed the page looking for the sentence he wanted. He explained the words of that famous sixteenth verse.

I would later find out that at the moment of salvation, many spiritual new-borns report exhilaration, euphoria, elation, even ecstasy. I felt none of those things. I didn't repent of any sin. I didn't cry a tear. I didn't even pray a prayer. I simply believed what my Dad told me about Jesus and His promise of eternal life. The moment passed without pomp or circumstance. Maybe the angels were singing, but I didn't. The gold-guided instant I became immortal faded into the hazy wake of distant recollection. I can hardly dust off the memory enough to recall any of the words spoken. I probably went right back to my crayon masterpiece on the floor.

Something new awoke in me that night, though it wouldn't be long before I became incredibly confused about the entire affair.

COLD CAT CASE

Grandma and Grandpa lived in Dallas. Our trips there often came in winter since the most active concentration of holidays accompany the cold weather. We would draw shapes in the fog our breath made on the van windows as we drove.

Being a kid who lived hours from my grandparents meant I was probably more attached to my pets than my parent's parents. We, the brothers, would rush from the van on return home in a mad competition to see who would first give Leo, our cat, the boyish affectionate aggression to which he was accustomed. Leo had endured tremendous tribulation under the iron hand of our villainous triumvirate. Aluminum foil hats, rubber bands on the paws, and pillowcase kidnappings were some of our favorite tortures that we inflicted upon him.

Leo was the best kind of cat. He was big and unthreatened by our boyish antics. He endured each of our loving experiments without bitterness or contempt. He was always ready for some lap time, a scratch, or a bedtime snuggle.

By the time the wheels hit the end of the driveway, the side door on our blunt-nosed Nissan van was already sliding free. The brothers and I fanned out in an eager search party for our black-furred companion. A short search was all it took before we lost interest. Cats can hide for weeks in a cinder block. No point wasting sunlight. If Leo needed some solitude, we'd leave him to it. It was nearly lunchtime, so our attention was quickly steered toward the fridge.

"I'll make lunch," Mom called from the screen doorway.

After carrying my coat to my room, removing my shoes, and reacquainting myself with my Lego collection, I returned to the kitchen to await the mid-day meal. I crawled into the bay window seat next to Levi when I noticed both of my brother's staring in Mom's direction. She was standing at the stove, warming a pot of tomato soup. Tears were streaming down her face. My brothers and I looked at each other, not sure what to do. I was the designated club spokesperson for our three-member group, so I got up and approached.

"Mom, why are you crying?" I said cautiously.

"Go out and ask Dad," she said. I looked back to the brothers as we all shuffled to the door. A perimeter search revealed that Dad was in the backyard, shovel in hand, digging a hole. A small but growing pile of red clay sat next to the depression where he was working.

We had a neighbor at the time who was about eighty years old. She had smoked heavily all her life, and her health was failing. Since my brothers and I had often played with her grandkids, my parents felt the need to prepare us for Mrs. McCullough's soon expected death. They did this with periodic talks about mortality. They had explained that Mrs. McCullough was elderly, and death is a natural part of life.

With these discussions still ringing the bells of my mind and the shovel in Dad's hand, I began to piece together the puzzle. As I watched Dad lift each shovel full of dirt from the ground, the truth dawned on me. Mrs. McCullough had died, and Dad was digging a grave to bury her in our backyard. I was sure of it.

I spent my free time playing in that backyard, and it caused all kinds of prickly emotions to think of Mrs. McCullough laid to rest beneath my active feet. "Are you going to bury Mrs. McCullough there?" I asked. I was not so much asking whether he was going to bury the neighbor in our yard, but why he had to do it where we played.

"No, Son. Of course not," he said. He struck a few more shovelfuls before the hole was complete. Mrs.

McCullough would certainly not fit. There must be some other reason. Although he had no tears, he was reluctant to fill us in on why he needed to dig. After a resolved sigh, he speared the shovel into the dirt and turned his attention to his three clueless sons.

"Mr. Jones came down a few minutes ago." Dad said. Mr. Jones was the father of our best friend in the neighborhood named John. He had volunteered to feed Leo while we were out of town. Dad gestured to a shoebox I had not previously noticed as he continued. "He came down to feed the cat and found him dead next to his food bowl."

Lance, the oldest, understood first. His sobbing began the chain reaction. In seconds our faces were streaked and our shoulders bounced with rhythmic weeping. "Mr. Jones said that he found a dead bee lying next to Leo. He thought that Leo may have been stung and was allergic." Dad reached for the shoe box and stepped toward the tiny grave he had prepared. Lance was the first to speak.

"Can we pet him one last time?" Lance bellowed between sobs. A dad's desire to give solace to his sobbing sons is strong. He pulled the lid from the box and held it out so that we each might stroke our feline friend one final time.

"Ahh, why is he hard?" Lance said as his hand grazed the lifeless body that felt like cold stone. He recoiled at the sensation, but then reached in for further inspection. Apparently, Mr. Jones had stored Leo in his deep freezer as a preservative until we returned from our trip. That lit off another powder keg of wailing. We each reached in eagerly now as much out of curiosity. We stroked the cat-sicle for a brief moment before Dad decided that it wasn't helping.

We watched as Dad piled dirt on top of Leo's chilled corpse. We made a poorly crafted cross to serve as a grave marker. We went in to eat tomato soup. We sat around the table crying. We had met death and the meeting left us all feeling frigid.

It was around that time that I realized I was going to die. The relationship between the cold cat case and my understanding of impending mortality is unmistakable. If it could happen to Leo, it could happen to me. Someday, possibly soon, I would be placed in a deep freezer while my hole was being dug, or at least that is how I imagined it. I began to think often of death. Deep stabbing questions grew like stalactites in the icy cave of my mind.

What happens after I die? I thought. I thought of the moment I had heard the gospel at Dad's drawing table. I had believed, but would that be enough? Wasn't there something I was supposed to do? I was looking for a sure way to hedge my bets on eternity. I needed assurance. *How could I be sure I was saved?*

"Do you want to go to Todd's church this evening?" Mom asked one Sunday afternoon, phone held to the side of her head. The winter days were giving up their chill to the spring thaw. The memory of Leo was still vivid, but its chilly sting had blunted. Todd was the kid who lived next door. I'd never been to his church. In fact, it hadn't even occurred to me that he and his family attended.

"Uhh, yeah, I guess so," I said, not quite sure what I agreed to. Todd was more popular at school, and I was happy to have the invitation. I was intimidated to imagine what I would see there. Their baby blue minivan stopped in front of the house about fifteen minutes later.

Their church was not like the little Bible church my family attended. Theirs had a pipe organ, red velvet pews, and a tall stage-bound pulpit made of some dark engraved wood. The ceiling was so high the room could have had clouds. Todd seemed bored, but I was mesmerized. The pipes echoed in the room and vibrated the brass chandeliers. The organist's hairdo could have housed at least twelve squirrels, but they would have been unhappy with the way it wobbled while she played. The preacher hollered as if the entire congregation was hard of hearing, even though he had a microphone that worked just fine as far as I could tell. That night I was introduced to what I'd later come to know as an 'altar call.' The service ended with the suited man passionately begging his listeners to get their sins forgiven.

Are my sins forgiven? I wondered. I had believed what my Dad had told me at his drawing table a few years earlier, but I couldn't remember asking for forgiveness. I pondered what I had seen and heard on the drive back that evening. I returned home with more questions than answers.

"Lord, please forgive me for my sins." I started to pray like a mantra as I laid in bed. I repeated it every night. I still remember the mental image that came when I would pray this. I was moving down a road. On the side of the road was sign after sign. Each one said, *ask for forgiveness again.* No matter how far I traveled down this road, there were more signs. I could see them in the distance stretching over the horizon. I felt trapped. Nightly I begged to be absolved, but the weight of not knowing whether I'd been forgiven was heavy.

This sinister fear sprouted quickly from somewhere deep within. I seriously doubted that my sins were forgiven. Thus I prayed more passionately each night repeating the phrase like a rosary. For months, maybe even years, I begged God for forgiveness. I was mortified of facing death without having righted my sin problem.

The doubt sunk its black roots into my soul. I believed that Jesus *could* forgive me, but I was afraid that I hadn't prayed the prayer right, or I didn't mean it, or if I meant it, I didn't want it bad enough. Viney tendrils of fear followed the fractures downward and did their best to soak up any living water in the well of my being. No matter how hard I prayed, I doubted more and more.

CHURCH OF THE PHDS

Before city council decided to build the bypass, a multi-mile loop around my hometown, much of the outskirts were still blanketed by the pine forest of East Texas. The little Bible church we attended was a metal building at the end of a dead-end road, surrounded by tall pines. The church attracted an enlightened lot, as could be seen by the highly educated congregation who faithfully attended. We had multiple doctors that taught Sunday school; a dentist did the announcements, college professors led the songs and ran the youth group. There were an unusual amount of Ph.D.'s for the size of the church.

My perception of church was synonymous with high education. We were as likely to learn how to parse Greek verbs as we were to get a lesson on the basics of the gospel. The Jr. High Sunday school class had a fat packet of homework weekly. Me and my friend Ashley, the daughter of a Lawyer and a Doctor, were the only ones in our Sunday class who even attempted the workload. By the time I was in 6th grade, the small youth group allowed Jr. High kids to participate. The curriculum for the youth group was a video series from the '60s by Francis August Schaeffer, a famous knicker wearing philosopher who also had a Ph.D., of course.

We had bought into the allure of complexity. We considered ourselves to be a church that went 'deep.' This left the impression that other churches in town were shallow and didn't understand the Bible.

"Will Brian go to Hell?" I asked Dad one summer afternoon. Brian was a friend from school who attended another more 'shallow' denomination. The subject of other churches was not brought up often at our church, but anytime it did arise, it was in hushed condescending tones. I had surmised that most churches were filled with people who were headed toward the lake of fire. After all, if everyone in every church was saved, then shouldn't we all meet together? I don't know if I was concerned for Brian's soul, or if I was just wondering if I ought to look down on him as well.

"Why don't you have a conversation with Brian about that?" Dad suggested. What a novel idea? Talk *to* Brian, instead of *about* Brian. I could just ask him... I could say... uh... or maybe I could tell him... well...

what? What was I supposed to say? I never talked to Brian about his eternal destiny. I avoided having that soul-saving conversation because I wasn't sure how to verify whether Brian had done what was required. I don't know if it was due to my church experience or not, but despite the heavy emphasis on academic study of the Scripture, I was really confused.

It's funny how certain daydreams from childhood stand out. One such mental meandering happened on an otherwise unmemorable evening that same summer. I would often spend the last few minutes before bedtime next to Mom, who ended her day reading in bed. I'd love to say I sat there and read, but my plan was much more sinister. I knew that if I were to lay in just the right place where her arm was not too strained, she would give me a back scratch. For me, a back scratch was the closest thing I ever got to hard drugs. I was hooked, and Mom was my dubious dealer. If her hand slowed, I would give a mild spasm to remind her that I was awake and expectant. She never complained or protested; what an enabler.

One evening as I was lying there having my back flesh filleted from the bone, I was considering what I knew about the gospel. Proudly, I thought I knew quite a lot. Certainly more than Brian, maybe even as much as Ashley, though she was better than me at spelling and punctuation. Despite all, I knew there was still something disjointed. There was something that didn't make sense to me. I had not yet wrestled my uncertainty about forgiveness into submission, and that left me open to a host of other doubts.

"If I could come up with a better way to explain the gospel, it would make me famous," I said to myself, glad that my mom couldn't hear my inner monologue. It was a fleeting thought, a passing whisper in my mind, though it illustrates how confused and frustrated I had become. I was unsatisfied with my understanding of the gospel. Even at that young age, I dreamed of having a different and clearer mindset, although my motivation for fame and recognition was certainly a sin, and I'm embarrassed even to record it here. The reason I do is that it was evidence of a growing chasm between my understanding and assurance. I wanted certainty and assurance, but I wasn't finding it in the academia of the Bible teaching church I attended.

"How do I know I'm saved?" I asked Dad a few days later. The out-of-the-blue questions were something Dad looked forward to. Being a college professor and a father of three bright-eyed boys, he lit up anytime a question was asked. He knew just where to turn in his well worn Bible.

"Look here," he said as he pointed. "Read that." I was a little reluctant and didn't enjoy being put on the spot. I complied though, knowing he had some wisdom to impart.

"I write these things to you who believe in the name

of the Son of God so that you may know that you have eternal life." I got through it shakily. My remedial reading class paid off.

"What do you see there?" Dad asked. I scanned it again, trying to understand why he had brought me to this particular sentence. When I didn't get it right away, he dropped his finger to the verb, which was begging for my attention. "What's that word?"

"Know," I said tentatively.

"That's right. John is explaining that it's possible to *know* that you have eternal life." He let that sink in for a moment. I thought about my nightly prayer ritual. I thought about my doubt while lying on Mom's bed. I thought about my frustration with the complexity of the Bible teaching I was receiving. He waited for it all to process.

"I don't feel like I know," I shuffled. "I mean, how do I know for sure?" He talked me through it once more. The discussion was not so different from the night he introduced me to John 3:16. Words like believe, and faith swirled in the air like an aromatic plume from an extinguished candle. He could tell I was still struggling even as we talked. As the discussion came to a close, he gave a suggestion.

"Why don't you talk to your Bible study leader about it?" Dad said. No doubt, he thought my small group facilitator would support and enhance the presentation he had given. I took his advice.

The week was slow in rolling. I continued to beg for forgiveness nightly just in case I died in my sleep. Our groups met on Sunday nights which might as well have been a decade away. My memory is hazy, but I bet we were studying Leviticus in original Hebrew, like every other youth group in town. I waited until Bible study was over, and all of my friends had left. I didn't want Ashley or any of the other smart kids to hear the dumb question I was about to lay on our leader. With a tremble in my voice and a knot in my stomach, I spoke.

"How do I know that I'm saved?" I said, clearly embarrassed to be asking fundamental questions. This was the church of the Ph.D., and I felt like the lone dummy. My leader closed his Bible and gave me his full attention. I could sense that the wait was over. He would give a concise and profound answer whose pithy truth would end my journey.

"The fact that you are asking these types of questions is probably a good sign," he said as he gathered some papers and glanced at the door.

"Yes, and?" I wanted to say but waited silently for more. He tucked his oversized Bible under his arm and gave me a look that said, *are there any other questions?* I was still waiting for his wisdom when I realized he had just provided it. His insight was about as useful as wet Kleenex. His answer to the eternal security question was, "Asking these questions is probably a good sign."

"Oh, OK," I said sheepishly, pretending as if his

words were something other than a slap in the face. What a dangling carrot— I might be saved simply because I wanted to know how to be saved. A desire not to go to the lake of fire was a good sign and might mean I won't. That's very reassuring, thanks a lot, buddy. I was so embarrassed and dissatisfied by the whole thing that I stopped asking that question altogether. I folded it in on itself and buried it deep. It smoldered there, sending up blackened acrid smoke signals in the years that followed.

THE WILD WOODS

As we grew into devious little miscreants, we could feel the blisters brought by the struggle against our behavioral constraints. With each wriggle, they grew tighter. There were rules at home, rules at school, and rules on the playground. There were even rules for proper bathroom etiquette. Didn't they know I was a descendant of rugged and powerful men who shaped the western frontier with their bare hands? Didn't they realize I came from a long line of hunters, builders, explorers, and warriors? Where can a boy go to get away from the stifling congestion of rules and regulations? That was a question that most boys of my generation faced. Some found solace in sports; others escaped into video games. I was a terrible athlete, and video game consoles were too expensive for my family's budget.

The girls I knew seemed fine with the life they had been dropped into, even elated to follow the strictures of small-town etiquette. It seemed like school, church, and dinner table behavior was designed by girls for girls. The dads would leave and be gone all day doing man stuff. I wanted to do man stuff. My brothers and I wanted nothing more than to be set free from the handcuffs of modern behavior. We didn't just want to throw the rulebook out the window; we wanted to set it on fire and chuck it through the shattered glass of a fast-moving car we'd stolen from the neighbor's grandma. We could feel the creaking of our joints as we grew to be giants, in a structured cell far too small.

The place we found our liberation was a small patch of woods that dead-ended our street. The roughly paved road descended into a wild pinewood forest. Developers had likely passed over it when planning the neighborhood because it had an iridescent stream that oozed with oily orange water year-round. Even to this day, cartographers have never given the trickling brook a name. It was a wilderness of boyhood passions away from the intrusive eye of groaning grown-ups. The creek was more our home during those barefoot Texas summers than the house at which we held official residence. For us, the creek and surrounding woods were a magical land.

On exiting the ordinary world of Eastridge Drive, we would utter the magical phrase, "we're going to the creek." The gate master, Mother, would allow passage, seeing an opportunity for a few minutes of quiet. These words would transport us to a mysterious world that did not exist in the same dimension as the one of rules, homework, and bathroom etiquette. On saying this magical incantation, we might appear in the northeast province, which was known as "the ramps." It was a red clay basin where previous generations of boy builders had constructed a mighty array of bike ramps. Much of it lay in ruins by our era.

We might be whisked away instead to the cliffs, a territory where the creek's oxbow had carved out a twelve-foot outcropping off of which we often ghosted our bikes. On saying so, we might instead find ourselves as deep in the woods as "Doug's," a dangerous realm of private property where a mean troll with a four-wheeler and a BB gun lived. Though all of these magical regions were well known to the pack of boy explorers, these might as well have been foreign lands as far as my parents were concerned. That was the first real freedom we took as boys. Each time we stepped into the magical world of "the creek," we were no longer tied to the mundane drudgery of proper behavior.

There were such magical treasures buried like ancient secrets in those woods. A half-century of boys had grown to men playing among those trees and had left the debris of adolescence behind for us to discover, use for a while, and return to the creek's shores so the next generation of boyish explorers could come of age.

The most significant discovery was that of the Grand Ax Of Nameless Creek. It spawned legendary lore of mythic proportions on par with those of King Arthur's famed Excalibur. My older brother Lance— we shall call him Sir Lancelot— was exploring the shore of the muddy creek bereft of security. Though he was a mighty warrior in heart and valor, he longed for the feel of cold steel against his palm, yet no worthy weapon could be found to match his wit and skill. Standing next to the raging river, he beckoned the Lady of the Creek to bring forth a mighty ax, so with it, he should smite his enemies with the mighty smitery of his smiting hand. The Lady of The Creek, in shimmering light, cast a golden sunbeam through the dappling trees upon something buried within the mud. A brilliant ax rose up out of the water. As Lancelot reached for the weapon, a voice from the water sang, "You shall henceforth wield this Grand Ax and always its grip you shall feel. Until once again, the Lady of the Creek shall reclaim the ancient steel."

Ok, that's not exactly how it happened, but it might as well be as far as memory serves. Actually, I couldn't remember how we found it, which is why I recently asked Lance how he discovered the hatchet: that's right it wasn't really an ax. His direct quote was much less legendary. He said, "I just saw something in the mud by the creek. It was the color of the rock, but it was shaped wrong, so I picked it up. It was really rusty." Though his version is more accurate, I like my memory of the glowing ax provided by the magical Lady of the Creek. In fact, there is more to the tale.

After years of using and benefiting from the magic in the ax, the Lady of the Creek knew, in her wisdom, we were growing too old to wield it much longer. She knew we would soon outgrow the mysterious land, and thence never again return to the magical realm. With a shimmering song, she beckoned to the ax, calling it back to that dark brook. As often is the case, the warrior who had grown attached resisted, trying to keep the ax for himself. Yet after many tears, the young troubadour returned to the Lady of the Creek. Bearing the ax upon the waters, he relinquished his mighty grip and watched it slowly sink beneath. The Lady of the Creek reclaimed the much-loved weapon thence safeguarding it until another worthy warrior of the wood might come.

I really wish that is how it happened, though I think Lance would tell it differently. He'd say, "We lost the hatchet when I accidentally dropped it in a deep part of the creek, and we couldn't find it." Coincidence, you say? No! It was magic.

DARK MAGIC

That hatchet was the second installment of our freedom plan. We cut trees and warded off wild beasts with it. We were men with the power to build or destroy. We could finally challenge the troll and fell timber. Each night before we returned to the ordinary world, we would hide it in a safe place and return to it the next day. It was amazing to have this shared legend. We saw it as a gift from above. It was the first big secret we kept from our parents, but it would not be the last.

There was another kind of magic we found in those woods. It was dark magic, so black the sun would dim, and our hearts would turn to stone. Its siren call beckoned. Its inky spell would bind to us like tar.

One day when walking among the trees with my little brother Sir Levi, our eyes were at once cast upon a scrap of parchment near the creek with no name. The hairs on the back of my neck immediately began to stand on end and my spine tingled. I sensed in my spirit that there was some dark magic at play. I reached for a switch and tore it asunder. With the twig, I made to poke at the parchment with its woody tip. I sought to discover of what sort was the mysterious scrawl.

"Don't look," I said at once to my brother. "This is dark magic." For my brother, Sir Levi was younger than I. He had not yet felt the quickening of the dark arts as I had.

"What is it?" he asked as I attempted to turn the page over with the twig.

"It is an enchanted parchment. It comes from the library of that foul wizard known as Hugh Hefner." Levi leaned in to take a closer look. Even then, I could feel the magic working on me as well.

"Of what sort of magic is this?" he asked.

"Mind magic," I replied, now feeling the trance setting in. "It enchants the viewer with a deep seed of desire. The poor soul whose eyes so much as glance at this parchment will henceforth be drawn by dark impulse to see more. The magic pulls at the heart and clouds out the light of reason. There are those so captured by this dark wizard's spell that they spend their lives seeking more and more parchments until they have lost everything in the gloomy pursuit."

Sir Levi and myself fought the spell, though I feared its shadowy fingers had already clawed their way into the crevices of our minds.

"We must bury it at once," I proclaimed. "We must bury it so that no unwary traveler becomes bewitched as we have now become."

Thus, we plunged the parchment beneath the water, leaving it to the Lady of the Creek. We hid it from the view of any passerby hoping beyond hope that it would be enough to save a single innocent bystander from befalling our foul fate.

Oops, I did it again. I keep making legend of my childhood. I think if my brother were to remember this, which he probably doesn't because he was young, he would tell it differently. I wish that it were a fairy tale. I wish that it was a magical quest that had a final and extraordinary conclusion. In the storybooks, there is always a simple answer. This is not one of those storybooks. The reality is not nearly so magnificent.

The truth behind the legend is this: while walking in the woods with my little brother, we found a single page from a pornographic magazine. The women on the page were otherworldly. The memory is a blur, as if my mind censored the images on those glossy pages. Somehow I knew I ought not touch the scrap as if its filth might be transferred to my fingertips as a black smudge forever. What I didn't realize is that my eyes were the portal by which the damage entered my soul. Within a few seconds, we had shoved it beneath the water with a stick trying to get it out of view. Though, the sinister result I carry in my mind even still. I felt conflicted about it. I had sensed that it was wrong. However, I had seen my first naked lady, and I was hooked.

BIBLE BY NIGHT LIGHT

My fourth-grade class was buzzing with Christmas time enthusiasm. The whir of exuberant voices filled the room as a holiday coloring sheet went around. The Christmas break was coming, with its presents and candy. The page slid into place as I reached under my desk for my crayons. Some kids had the 48 color set, but mine was a simple box well worn and doubly used. A deluxe selection of coloring sheets offered a myriad of options: Christmas bells, Santa Clause, or reindeer. As the sheets hit desks, the scratch of colored wax on paper began to fill the room.

I glanced at Michael, the kid who was seated directly across from me. He stared at the page, crayons in hand. He looked at the sheet as if it held images of kittens being ground into cat meat sandwiches. I glanced at the sheet in front of him to find that it was the same. I looked at mine, trying to understand the offense. Whatever the problem was, it was not evident to me. He turned toward the teacher as if to say something.

"Oh, sorry, Michael. I forgot," She said before he could protest. She flitted over to her supply closet and retrieved a blank piece of paper and traded it for Michael's. When the offending sheet had been removed, he set to work, drawing with crayons on a completely blank canvas. As expected, his picture was not Christmas themed.

"Are you Jewish?" A kid asked Michael on the playground later that week.

"I'm Jehovah's Witness," he said. "But we call ourselves JW's for short." He was not afraid to talk about his faith and had obviously been trained well to do so. We had become friends, but there were a host of mysteries that surrounded him.

One of the things I loved about Michael was his uncanny wit, especially for a fourth-grader. He read fat fantasy books even at that age. We both were good artists, always drawing in our free time. At lunch, he would sculpt his mash potatoes into Hoover Dam with the gravy as the reservoir. He'd have me look as he cried, "The dam is going to blow!" A flow of gravy would pour into the valleyed plateau of his plate.

He invented an imaginary game we played at our desks. He called it "war." We would use pretend weapons on each other while the teacher was talking. If I pointed a make-believe pistol, he would have to upstage it with a pretend shotgun. At that point, I'd have to retrieve my bazooka. He'd pull out a Howitzer. It progressed until he would blast us both to dust by deploying a thermonuclear weapon right there at our desks. You can imagine how much trouble we got into using nukes indoors.

As the year progressed, it was becoming more obvious that he was different from everyone else. He would not place his hand over his heart or recite the pledge. He would not take part in any patriotic or holiday-themed activities. He was an impressive kid, standing his ground against teachers and other pushy students. The guy was made of solid steel.

I lost touch with him for a few years until we reconnected in eighth-grade art. We would often skip class and wander the school. We were not the average trouble makers, though. We had hall smarts. One time when we were skipping, we saw the school principal walking our way. Most kids would run, right? Not us. We walked right up to the principal and asked a deceptively clever question, "Mr. Stevens, do you know where Mrs. Smith is? She's not in her class or her office." At first, it may not seem intelligent, but here's the trick. We hadn't lied; we implied. There was no lie needed; we simply implied that we were on an errand involving a faculty member, which we weren't. The principal pointed us down the hall and told us to look in that direction. Then if a teacher stopped us, we could legitimately say, "We were sent down here by Principal Stevens." All this without a single lie. After this little maneuver, we would slap high fives and brag on ourselves to ourselves. "We could talk our way out of a Chinese prison," he once claimed.

We were unlike class-cutters in another way. Most kids that cut class would go out back and smoke cigarettes or something more illegal. We weren't interested in that. We would cut class and have religious discussions. He—being a Jehovah's witness—had vastly different views about Jesus and salvation. Our debates were friendly, but we were both trying to evangelize the other. It was out of mutual friendship and compassion that we cut class and debated.

"I don't want you to go to Hell," I'd say.

"I don't believe in Hell," he'd reply.

"Well, I mean, I want you to be saved."

"I'm obeying what the Bible tells me to do, aren't I? Why don't you think I'm saved?" He'd say calmly, and he had a point. He was incredibly focused on obedience. He was devoted to the point of being ostracized by his peers, and yet he didn't give in. He was more bold about his faith than I was. If works could save someone, I suspect he'd be the first in line. He was a better representative of his religion than I was of mine, and yet I dared to tell him he wasn't saved. Honestly, I felt conflicted about it. I wasn't sure why he wouldn't be saved, other than my church leaders had told me Jehovah's Witnesses are wrong.

"But God's salvation is—" and so it went. On and on and on. We continued these kinds of conversations throughout the year. We liked hanging out, but we couldn't do it outside of school because we were both so committed to our faith and our churches, respectively. The best way to get more friend time would be for one of us to be converted. However, no matter how hard we tried, neither of us budged an inch.

It was around this time I finally acquired my own bedroom, though I should say it was actually a converted entry hall and dining room. Privacy was a new commodity that I wasn't sure what to do with. The first night after bedtime, I shined a flashlight around the room to see what would happen. No police sirens or military helicopters swooped in. I would try something a little more daring the next night. It didn't take long before I became a stone-cold rebel. I could do whatever I wanted after bedtime as long it was in my room. My rebellion led me out of my bed each night. I would lay on the floor in front of the little orange night light, open my Bible, and read by the dim glow. Mwa hahaha. My parents never even knew about this dubious miscarriage of bedtime justice. I was reading my Bible after bedtime! They were clueless.

Initially, I was studying my Bible to debate Michael,

but the habit stuck. Really, I was excited to be reading my Bible on my own. For some reason, it just fit me. I didn't just read the easy stuff either; I tackled the biggies. I went through Leviticus right there under the night light. Romans and Hebrews were next. I was taking big gulps. It was exhilarating. I loved it.

I noticed something about the Bible. I didn't know how to make sense of what I noticed. My pastor and Sunday school teacher had told me that salvation is a free gift. However, what I saw in the Bible was a boatload of instructions and commands. Even the New Testament was packed with orders from on high.

I vaguely remember speaking this question aloud in the quiet of my dim bedroom, "If salvation is free, why are there so many commands in the Bible?" I knew what Michael would say to that, and at times I wondered if he might be right.

THE STOOL
METHOD

As my love for the Bible was beginning to blossom, my friendship with Michael was soon tested by fire. By eighth grade, Michael was reading the *Wheel of Time*. It's a huge series of fantasy novels, and each is as fat as a Webster's dictionary. Michael's face was buried in a book most of the time when he wasn't talking to me. Apparently, that's the universal target for a bully to pounce. One such bully caught the scent and made chase.

Ross was a good looking athlete who hit his growth spurt early and wasn't afraid to pick on kids that he deemed nonthreatening. He began in the first month of the school year, at first just taunting Michael with ever-increasing ploys. The torment became physical before long. Not only was Michael a book worm, but he was part of some "weird religion," according to Ross. This was all the license Ross needed to turn Michael's eighth-grade year into a hellish nightmare.

"What happened to your eye?" I asked one day at lunch.

"Ross happened."

"Seriously?" I said. His eye was red, and there was a cut on his temple.

"I'm going to have to do something," Michael said calmly. There was no emotion, just gut-level resolve. It was a simple calculation for him. He could see the trajectory of the situation, and it was becoming unbearable. I wasn't sure what he could do about it. His faith taught him to be nonviolent. Even if he was willing to be violent, Ross was huge and pretty dangerous. "If I don't it's just going to get worse."

Fourth-period science class was the only class other than art, which Michael and I shared. Unfortunately, Ross also occupied a seat in the same room. We were working on an assignment, and Michael, like usual, was the first to finish. He had to walk by Ross' desk to turn in his paper. Ross spit on him as he passed and threatened him with some asinine violence. Michael didn't respond but simply walked away, or so Ross thought.

Michael stepped toward the teacher's desk, retrieved a heavy metal stool, lifted it high in the air, and let the heavy end fall on the crown of Ross' head. The sound of it made the whole class jump. Michael didn't say a thing; his action had spoken plenty loud. He stepped back, still holding the stool, not sure if his plan had worked. Ross stood from where he was sitting, shoved the desk out of the way, and squared off. He had fire in his eyes. Michael told me later he was thinking, *sheesh, I'm going to have to hit him again.* Fortunately, he didn't need to. A second passed, and the dizziness washed over Ross as blood began to gush down his face. He teetered and plopped back into his chair. Michael had gambled, and it seemed as if it may have paid off.

As Michael put down his stool, there arose a grumbling from some of Ross' buddies. They did not see Ross as the bested bully but instead the victim. It was a crime perpetrated by a bizarre and dangerous weirdo. They were enraged, and they too had fire in their eyes. The rabble-rouser, a skinny kid, named Josh said, "Y'all saw what he did to Ross. Let's get him." They apparently planned to gang up on Michael and beat him bloody before the Principal arrived.

That's when I entered the situation. I guess I didn't want to be left out of the beating because I stepped next to Michael, who still looked stunned at what he had done.

"Back off! Ross has been torturing him all year. Michael did what he had to to make it stop." I said. It was the adrenaline talking. The real me was hoping they weren't going to make me back up my words with my fists. I was willing, but they would have torn me and Michael apart. Though, no matter what they did, I'd be by Michael's side for the fray.

Fortunately, they did what I had told them to do. They backed off. That was probably because Ross was covered in blood by now. His shirt was soaked with the sticky crimson flow. We'd learn later that though there was plenty of blood, no longterm damage had been done.

The message was clear enough: "I will no longer be your punching bag!" He had finally spoken in a language Ross, and every other bully could understand. Ross never tormented him again. In fact, nobody ever bullied Michael after that.

I admired Michael's bravery, but his parents didn't seem to share that feeling. Up until the point Michael dropped the stool on Ross' head, I had not seen a crack in his morality. He was the most moral and faith-committed person I knew. Michael's parents' looked so forlorn when they arrived at the school later that day. How could their obedient son be caught up in something so criminal?

No doubt, Michael's act of violence was met with warnings from his Bible Study leader to stay on the straight and narrow. For sure, his devout parents reminded him of the dangers of violence and the possibility of straying from a righteous path. He could be shunned if he didn't get his life right. For them, there was no difference between being shunned by the church and being rejected by God. If Michael didn't repent and move in the right direction, then according to his church's theology, he could wind up unsaved.

He prayed for forgiveness for his violence even though he was convinced he did the right thing. He repented, and to my knowledge, he never harmed another person even to this day. He's still an active leader in the Jehovah's Witness church. It's funny to think that the Saturday after Michael had made his bully bleed, he was going door to door telling people about God's Kingdom plan, just like any other Saturday. He had to; his salvation required that he continue to obey God.

I refused to admit it, but in this way, Michael and I were really in the same boat. If I were to ask Michael, "Do you know for sure you are saved?" He would have had to respond with, "I won't know until the end of my life." If I were honest, I would have answered that question the exact same way. I knew I was supposed to know for sure that I had eternal life, but I wasn't sure how I was supposed to arrive at that conclusion. After all, what if I became a violent child abuser or a serial killer. What if I found out that I loved hurting people, left church altogether, and lived the rest of my life as an angry atheist? Wouldn't that mean that I was unsaved? Though Michael and I were from very different backgrounds and theological frameworks, we shared this one thing: We both had a lack of assurance. Neither of us evangelized the other because neither of us was inviting the other into anything more certain.

As Michael and I continued on to high school, we holstered our guns and settled into being friends who agree to disagree on theological matters. We grew tired of the constant debates which never seemed to lead anywhere. Though the question, like the wreckage after a storm, remained with me. How can I be sure I'm saved?

DRUGS FOR BOYS

Junior High sleepovers were the best of times and the worst of times. Our neighborhood was not lacking in options. John's house was always a safe choice, though he had a curly furred dog who demanded a crotch sniff followed by a face lick. Spending the night at Jimmy's was not bad because he had a Nintendo, but his mom's boyfriend and his curly mullet creeped us out. We never spent the night at Brian's though he invited us all the time. The choice location to spend the night was Todd's place. His parents were cool, there weren't any rules to speak of, he had a Nintendo, but we would learn that he had something no one else in the neighborhood possessed.

After school on Friday, we'd hit the streets on our bikes and round up the usual gang. We'd each hint around trying to get Todd to extend an invite. Todd was tired of his own house and preferred to stay with someone else, but he felt the pressure.

"We hardly ever spend the night at your place, Todd." Not true, but peer pressure isn't always truthful.

"Ok," he said with a smirk, knowing he had something new to show off to his friends. This night was different from all the ones that came before. Todd had something he had discovered, something he wanted to share with his buddies. We set up our sleeping bags in front of the game room TV. Todd made sure the door was locked and manned the remote as we bedded down for the night. He scanned the channels like he had severe ADHD.

"Just pick something already," someone protested. "Why do you keep changing the channel?" Todd ignored the chide. He was a man on a mission. About a quarter past midnight, his dizzying remote control work slowed. He finally came to rest on a movie, some low budget cop flick we'd never seen before. "Why'd you pick this? It looks super cheesy." We would soon see what Todd had on his mind.

The first thing I noticed was the language. I was used to the broadcast channels, which had tight wholesome censorship. No Sh's or F's sounded from our TV. Todd had brought us into the mysterious world of deep cable television. The language was not the only aspect that captivated us. The movie transitioned from police action on the streets to a couple in a bedroom. As the actress's clothes began to hit the floor, it was like I was suspended in a time warp, wrapped in a black hole. The quantum realm inverted. Electrons slowed around every atom of my body. The universe turned in on itself for 124 seconds of pure mental bliss.

I had seen nudity once before on a tattered scrap of a playboy magazine. The experience was nothing like this. It was as if part of me that I didn't know existed had just woken up for the first time, and it was hungry. After the scene concluded, I realized I had not taken a breath. It was an intense experience.

The invaluable commodity that Todd's house had that no one else's did was HBO. I left the next morning with a new awareness, something like a sixth sense. I wanted to see more. I'd go to bed for the dozen nights that followed, replaying the scene in my head. My daydreams had a new destination. Like a plant that bends toward the sun, my thought life arched every day a little bit more toward the erotic.

A few weeks later, we found ourselves spending another Friday night together, this time at John's house. John's dad had a job that required him to have the latest technology. At the time, the internet was becoming a household commodity. John's dad had a computer with a dial-up internet connection that clocked in at a smoking 96k bits per second. To put that in perspective, a typical internet speed today is 52,000k bits per second. Things have changed.

When we spent the night at John's, we slept in the office with his Dad's computer. Though John was uncomfortable with it from the beginning, we pressured him into getting on the internet. We had heard there was all kinds of filth for free.

With my brother and I over his should, John maneuvered through the seedy underbelly of the web. The final click began the download of a single nude photo. It came in blurry at first but slowly rendered pixel by pixel. Our hearts were beating through our chests as the image rastered. Once it did, there was a strange surprise.

I felt disappointed. The exhilaration I had experienced before wasn't present. The beast inside me was hungrier than he was the last time, and this wasn't enough. I wanted more. The growing pit in the center of my soul was yawning ever broader, darker, and deeper. This single image wasn't satisfaction. We began planning our next move when John made a quick maneuver with the mouse.

He closed the browser in a hurry. The startling motion made us jump. He shut down the computer and shoved his chair back from the desk. After standing, he faced my brother and I.

"We are never doing that again!" he said. His words were firm, forceful, and final. He had been there the night we spent at Todd's, and now he had been with us for our second hit of our new choice drug. With those definitive words, he let us know that that was where his involvement ended. Whatever dabbling, or more likely swimming, we did in the world of porn, John would not be there with us.

It wasn't until that moment that I realized what we were doing was wrong. Until this point, I had happened upon x-rated material without seeking it out. This was different. It had been deliberate. Here John drew the line. Unfortunately, I didn't have the strength of character to draw a line of my own.

We should have followed him. That night he proved himself to be a worthy leader. To my knowledge, he never struggled with the addiction. I wish I would have clung to him and his moral strength, but I was already too hooked to leave the stuff behind. The night John left porn behind, we should have celebrated for him, but we went to bed annoyed.

Being industrious, my brothers and I had learned to reprogram the family VCR. For those who don't know the acronym, it's the ancient equivalent to a DVR, kind of... It'd be too much to explain. Anyway, we figured out that we could get VH1, which was the off-brand version of MTV, by resetting the channel changer. Mom and Dad had intentionally left VH1 off the dial because it was sexually suggestive. In our endeavor to find more lewd eye candy, we stumbled upon what might as well have been an alien broadcast.

The cable box was programmed to skip channel

fourteen. When we reprogrammed the VCR, we scanned over it, not realizing what it was at first. It just looked like static. There were lots of static channels, so we didn't pay attention. Until one evening, when Mom and Dad weren't around, we rolled over it, and there was something in the static. Like finding out there is a voice in the sound of the ocean or a message written on the face of the moon, there were bodies in the static.

"It's a channel!" One of my brothers, exclaimed. "And they're—"

We leaned in to try and make sense of the white noise. Through the scratchy pattern, we could make out naked people, and they were doing... stuff. We had made the most dangerous discovery of our young lives. We were like kids who stumbled upon the recipe for dynamite. It was a channel that was partially scrambled, but it was clear enough for a trio of hormone-filled boys. It was our own pornographic treasure trove.

It wasn't long before we had friends over to our house to spend the night, though John wouldn't take part in it. I'm telling you, he was and is an impressive guy. The rest of us gorged on the static-filled indecency. The kinds of movies on this channel made HBO's selection look like Lifetime programming.

Things progressed from there. It wasn't long before it morphed from a curiosity shared by a few naughty boys into a private addiction. That was the first time I remember feeling the weight of cold black guilt. I knew I had given up part of myself, a part that was good, a part that I missed.

I ended my eighth grade year in depression. I just started crying one night. For the better part of a week, I would bellow around bedtime. I didn't want to be alone in my room, but I didn't want to be around anyone either.

"What's wrong, Honey," Mom asked when she noticed. I couldn't put accurate words to the emptiness. I felt isolated, like a kid who was no longer a boy but not worthy of being a man.

"I don't have any friends," I said. It wasn't true. I had some of the best friends in the world. I had friends that would die for me. I didn't know how else to put it into words. I had been marooned on a desert island. I had become isolated. It got so bad that Mom made me a sleeping pallet next to her bed. For two nights, I slept on the floor and held her hand as I cried myself to sleep. I never told her or anyone else about my new secret. She never knew about my new sin. Well, Mom, now you know.

JEFF'S NEW LIFE

Jeff was the crudest guy I knew. He could keep the whole lunch table laughing with his crass humor. It was sophomore year, and I had become fast friends with him. We both played in the marching band. Thus we spent most of our Friday nights and rehearsal times together. The more time I spent with Jeff, the more I worried about his soul.

He had grown up with kind, hard-working, albeit unchurched parents. His mom and dad were not concerned with matters of conservative morality. Jeff's high school girlfriend was often allowed to spend the night with their full awareness and blessing. Jeff was not particularly unhappy with the arrangement, but his marching band experience had introduced him to a large group of Christian buddies. Jeff noticed that his faith focused friends lived decidedly different.

"Want to skip band practice?" I asked Jeff one Tuesday morning. We had evening rehearsal that night, which was probably our director's one weekly chance to make us look less like a herd of feral cats on the marching field.

"Why?" Jeff asked.

"There is a big show at a church in Longview tonight, and I want to go. I thought you might like to come with me."

Although that was true, I wasn't giving Jeff all of the information. I didn't want him to know that I was terrified that he might go to Hell and I was trying to get him saved.

"Sure," he said. With that one word, the direction of his life was taking a turn, though he didn't know it. It was never hard to convince a friend to skip band rehearsal; the more difficult task was to convince the band director that it was worth the miss.

"Hey, Mr. Blackstone," I said a little bit nervous. "Me and Jeff have to miss band rehearsal tonight."

"Well, I hope you have a good reason." he said as his imperial stare drilled a hole through my face.

"I'm taking him to an evangelistic event," I said, but it didn't seem to be enough. "Lots of people are getting saved, and I want Jeff to see it." As soon as I said it, I wondered if I had made a strategic mistake? I didn't know if Mr. Blackstone was a believer, nor was I sure if that excuse would carry any weight.

"Well, that is a good excuse, " he said as he gave me a hardy slap on the shoulder and a brotherly grin.

The night came with more nerves. I asked Dad to give us a ride, and he was more than happy to oblige. Jeff sat in the back as the minivan rattled down the highway toward Mobberly Baptist Church. The event was to be a stage play frighteningly titled Heaven's Gates and Hell's Flames. I wrung my hands as we drove, afraid of what Jeff might think when he realized I was trying to get him saved. It felt like an ambush, and I was the Judas. But kind of like a reverse Judas—I don't know—Anyway…

We found our way to a velvety pew in the middle of the impressive sanctuary. As the lights went down, it was clear we were in for a real show. Dramatic music played as a series of tragic and unexpected deaths were depicted by amateur actors. Each would then be translated into the heavenly realm and made to stand before God. The recently deceased person would have to give a reason why they should be let into Heaven. Half the time, the dead person didn't make the cut and would descend into Hell to suffer torment forever.

What was stunning was that many of the characters thought they were saved for various reasons only to learn that God would not let them into Heaven. There were a few characters that believed but had not been fully committed in some way; even those believers went to Hell. The entire experience was overwhelming and instilled an incredible sense of doubtful dread in me. I can't imagine what it was doing to Jeff.

At the end, the pastor did an invitation to come down front and get saved. The man promised that anyone who came would be freed from the fear of Hell. Out of my peripheral, I could see that Jeff was on the edge of his seat.

"Do you want to go down?" I whispered. Jeff hesitated for a moment, though I could tell he wanted to move. "I'll go with you if you want," I added.

"Yeah," he said, as he rose mesmerized by what he had just seen. A large group migrated toward the stage together with us. Each person was in a post-show haze absolutely swimming in fear of Hell.

We were all ushered into a separate room. The volunteer staff divided us, which bothered me. An army of men and women with green name tags paired up with the new potential converts. Mine's name tag read 'Garry: counselor.' He seemed to be a little overeager in my estimation. I was made to sit down with the green name badge guy, and presumably, Jeff was made to do the same with his badged counterpart.

"Listen, Garry, I'm saved already, I just came down to bring my friend," I said as I scanned the room with my eyes. Jeff was seated about twenty paces away. I could see in the distance that he was fidgeting nervously. My explanation didn't phase Garry.

"So a rededication, then?" He said like a ray of

sunshine had just hit him in his tickle spot. He reached for his clipboard and marked a box with his freshly sharpened pencil.

"Uhh, no. I'm just here because—" I started to say.

"I'll pray a prayer, and you can repeat after me." He said with the kind of confidence that can only accompany a complete lack of self-awareness. This guy was going to get a notch on his belt even if he had to get rededicated on my behalf.

"I don't need—"

"Dear Lord," he said. Then he gave a long pause, obviously waiting for me to repeat. I stared at the top of his head for a moment before I reluctantly closed my eyes and began to repeat, annoyed, if only to get the whole thing finished.

"Thanks. See ya," I said when he had ended the prayer. The chair scraped the concrete floor as I stood abruptly and walked toward the nearest exit. I met Jeff on the other side. His experience was entirely different. Evidently, he had believed in Jesus for salvation. The counselor prayed with him and gave him a handful of materials to take home. I could tell that Jeff was excited as if a fifty-pound bag of bricks dropped from his shoulders. He was wearing this goofy grin.

I have to be honest, though. I was skeptical. After all, hadn't the play depicted a host of people who *thought* they were saved, but really weren't? How could I know for sure that Jeff had really been born again?

Was there a new spiritual life placed inside Jeff, or had he just been manipulated into coming down front and pressured into a ritual by a guy with a badge? I wrestled with these feelings not because I doubted the sincerity of Jeff's experience, but because I was confused.

"Well, I got saved," Jeff said with a smirk as we arrived back at my dad's minivan. Dad was surprised, probably wondering if this was one of Jeff's silly jokes. By the time the seatbelt snapped, Dad could see that Jeff was serious. I climbed in the front seat and shared an expeditious glance with Dad, quietly confirming what had happened.

"You know," Dad said as he put the keys in and turned over the engine. "A great next step would be to begin studying the Gospel of John together." As soon as the words escaped Dad's mouth, a knot twisted in my stomach. I had gotten the guy saved, wasn't that enough. Was I now supposed to do a Bible study? It was turning out to be a lot more work than I wanted.

I didn't take Dad's advice. I didn't study the Bible with him. I didn't invite him to church. I only occasionally talked to him about spiritual matters, but that only while at school. Jesus told Peter he would make him a fisher of men. Well, I had caught a fish, but I just dropped it on the shore and let it dry in the sun. I left Jeff to his own devices, something I'm incredibly embarrassed about now.

In the following months, I continued to wonder about the authenticity of Jeff's salvation. His habits stayed the same. His language didn't change. One positive turn was that Jeff was now attending his girlfriend's church. Though she also continued to attend his bedroom all night a few times a week. In virtually every conversion testimony I had heard, the person laid aside their old habits overnight. That didn't happen with Jeff, so what was I to think? How could Jeff 'really' be saved since he was still sinning so much?

My early reservation was later replaced with reassurance. With little to no help from me, Jeff began to win his battles with his old self. They were slight changes at first. He stopped using the F word, or he chose not to tell a disgusting joke. In time he even broke up with his girlfriend to purify his life. The gradual shift was comforting. Before long, I stopped worrying that Jeff would go to Hell. I settled into the idea that Jeff had really received salvation that night, but that realization came with a more significant doubt.

I only became convinced that Jeff had become saved after his life was 'bearing fruit' as the old church hens would call it. So, when Jeff started doing good works, I stopped worrying about him, but it unearthed an inconsistency in what I believed. I would have aggressively argued that, theoretically, salvation is a free gift that one gets apart from works. Though, in actual practice, I had to admit that I didn't believe my friend was saved unless he did good works. It made me wonder what would happen to me if I stopped following Christ. Would that mean I was never saved in the first place? If so, then how could anyone know if they are saved at all?

As Jeff's faith grew, his lifestyle became more Christlike, but with that change, my own personal doubts about assurance and salvation increased.

CHARISMA

"I'm in a band, come see our show this Friday," I said as I handed a flyer to a girl I didn't know. 'LED in concert at the Java Jira,' it read in big, bold text. She glanced at it with curiosity and then at me. She was pretty. I hoped she would come. I hoped she'd come with other cute friends. I wanted recognition for the hours of songwriting, gig seeking, and garage practice sessions. In short, I wanted fame.

There was a mighty music scene in the little town where I grew up. That may not seem strange since most modern metropolises have a vibrant range of live music offerings. However, the population of Kilgore could fit in a high school football stadium. The plethora of rock bands in our tiny hamlet was impressive, especially considering that most of them were Christian bands. That was the post-grunge era, where the music was loud and unorganized. Flannel was the uniform, and the lyrics were indecipherable.

I have a youth minister friend who says that kids

don't play instruments anymore; they play video games. Why were there so many Christian bands in our area and era? At that time, the cool kids played sports; everyone else was in a band. My friends joked about how many bands I joined. I was a drummer, and drummers were in high demand. At one time, I kept the beat for six different rock 'n roll acts. There wasn't a night of the week that I wasn't sitting at my drum kit somewhere. It's a blur now.

The popularity of being in a rock band could probably be traced back to one hard-rock Christian band, which reached a measure of regional success throughout East Texas. Model #777 was the top Christian band East of Dallas. This band, like so many others, was made up of four charismatic and passionate guys. They loved rock 'n roll and they loved Jesus. It was a dynamite combination since most parents of high school kids would balk at the idea of releasing their little darlings to go to a rock 'n roll show. Oh, the horror of drugs, sex, and rock 'n roll was too much. Any motivated teen at that time could simply say, "Mom, I'm going to see a *Christian* band."

"Oh, ok, Honey. Have fun. Don't come home before 3 am."

The four horsemen of this flagship rock band were scene builders. They were master hype men. They believed in their product and they knew how to sell it. The first time I saw them live I was mesmerized. They had the best stage show of any in the area. They had theatrical haze, an impressive light show, an automatic bubble maker, and a homemade machine that dropped glitter as they jammed. They even had a fifteen-foot crown of thorns that hung over the stage and shook like an earthquake when they let loose a face-melting solo. They held a captive audience spellbound for ninety solid minutes. Afterward, they left us wanting more. Though it might sound silly now, it was inspiring.

It wasn't long before there was a wave of others, reaching for the elusive commodity of local fame. My brothers and I were swept up in the frenzy and found ourselves shirtless and sweating on the various stages that were available for amateur Christian bands. Our band, like most, was not as good as the original, but it didn't seem to matter. What we lacked in quality we made up for with sheer ear-splitting volume. Our promise to the audience was an hour of mind-numbing noise and permanent hearing damage to remember us by.

Around a smattering of Christian bands formed a fickle audience of local fans who could be found Friday and Saturday nights at the local Christian venues, which were mostly churches. The churches allowed these loud, raucous nights in hopes of attracting the deafened masses of teens to their Sunday morning services. By and large, the high schoolers of the area were happy enough to attend the rock show but were not interested in becoming Sunday's pew sitters.

Even though the sheep scattered more than they grazed, a handful of churches were able, with near-magical resolve, to convert the Friday attendees to Sunday church-goers. Without exception, the key was to turn Sunday morning into a rock show as well. The church leadership of some more flexible congregations extended the concert and filled their liturgical stages with the young men and women that had rocked out the night before.

The churches that could endure the volume were the most charismatic in the area. Thus the kids who converted from concert-goers to church attendees found themselves in churches that sold a markedly more emotional brand of Christianity. Those teens that churches were able to retain were drawn in by moving services in which worshipers were told to feel more, press in, love God deeper, and other buzzy catchphrases. The entire emphasis was on one's ecstatic experience with God, and this approach gave very little time to biblical exploration. That was a kind of faith I was not at all familiar with, but these were my friends.

I visited one such church called Rock Hill. The name was fitting since it was both on a hill and offered a rock style service. At first, I found it strange that they did their services on Friday night. By the end, I understood. It was high entertainment on par with the theater or a sporting event. The ceremony began with prayer—no problem—though, I wasn't fond of holding hands and rocking back and forth with complete strangers. Next, while still holding hands, the congregation danced around the room. Imagine a conga line set to the worship tune; *Better Is One Day*. Then those who were most moved began shivering, shaking, and convulsing. They fell on the ground. A 'holy' blanket was placed upon their still convulsing body. Heaven forbid a person prone to seizures attend such a service. No one would ever know they were having an authentic medical emergency. Then those who were not slithering serpentine across the floor began babbling in what I'd describe as ecstatic gibberish. By this time, I found myself sitting in the back pew with a withdrawn look painted surreptitiously across my face.

"Come look outside," a sweating, red-face man shouted into the silence between a couple of the songs. He then explained, "It's nothing but rain clouds all around us, but God has opened the skies right above the church."

Many rushed outside, including me, though reluctantly. I heard mumblings even among the most devout, that his sky sight wasn't exactly accurate. It was a solid block of black cloud cover by the time I cast my eyes to the heavens. Maybe my faith wasn't strong enough. I left that night feeling confused about what I'd seen. I wasn't pulled in by the charisma of the scene, but I had to admit these people were excited about their faith. It was a kind of excitement that I didn't know how to share.

"Look at my filling," a friend said the next week. He was a regular attendee of Rock Hill's services. "God did a miracle and turned my fillings gold." I peered into his gaping mouth, a cavern with coffee laden breath. All I saw was black fillings that covered his back two molars. I leaned in, thinking that a miracle of God should be more obvious. This was not.

"Uh-huh," I said, not wanting to disagree with what he thought was a miraculous dental visit. Others were not so placating as I. Before long he stopped claiming the miracle. The irony was that he was the only one who was physically unable to see the supposed gold guided miracle. Nonetheless, he was the most convinced, at least for a while.

There were a lot of young people in those years who hopped on the emotional bandwagon, but that wagon was one driven by feelings and mysticism. This group of exuberant teens made Christianity a popular option at Kilgore High School. Though, the evangelism that was done by them was as much an invitation into the music scene as it was an invitation to believe.

There were undoubtedly people who not only believed but committed their lives to discipleship, but many never really went that far. In the years after high school, I watched many of these friends drop out of a life of faith. In time these fervent young men and women who seemed to be giants of the faith began to dissolve. Within a few years, many had left it all behind.

In the frenzy and excitement, I often felt like an outsider. My faith was different from many other's in that mine was hardly a passionate one. I rarely experienced elation concerning the Bible, God, or the Christian way of life. The new theology was this: *Real* Christians feel… something… anything. That was the overarching theme of East Texas Christianity among my peers. Whether or not someone was a Christian seemed to be based on whether or not they were experiencing intense zeal for God and Christ. There was little distinction between being 'on fire for God' and being saved. The inverse was then true too. If one was lukewarm, there was a real question about their eternal salvation. It was doing invisible damage to us that I would not understand for years to come.

In the following decade, a gob of those who came to faith during that time felt their passion fading. As the amber twilight began to lower on these soft souls going into the world, it became apparent that they had not been prepared to maintain a meaningful faith through trials. As soon as they moved off and went to college, started soul-sucking jobs, and raising kids, many experienced the waning of their faith. They no longer had the excited network of ardent friends. As a result, a sizable percentage no longer identify with the Christian faith. Many are even atheists now. How could they continue? If the teaching was—"Christians have passion!"—what are they supposed to think when their passion dissolved? The damage of this emotive-centric theology kept their roots so shallow that they were choked out by the weeds of the real world.

I got caught in the awkward double thought of it all. I was not inclined to agree with the emotion=faith equation, but it was hard to stay utterly undaunted by the colossal implications. Considering that I have the emotional depth of a boiled egg, I always felt insecure by my lack of emotion. I was too honest to pretend to be experiencing something if I wasn't. On a good day, I wondered why I couldn't feel what everyone else seemed to be feeling. On a bad day, I wondered if my lack of zeal might be due to a lack of salvation.

GARAGE STUDY

It was just going to be a small get together and at first, that's all it was. I had invited Stephanie, James, Jeff, and a few others. We met in my parent's garage where our band practiced. Amidst the ragged drum kit and second-hand electric guitars, we read a little bit of Ephesians together. I gave a few ideas that stood out to me from the verses. That was it. You couldn't really call it a Bible study, though those who came seemed happy enough. They hung around for an hour or so afterward.

The next week, we had to round up more chairs. The gathering had more than doubled. High school kids are like planets—they have gravity. The more mass you put together, the more others will be attracted. At the second garage meet-up, I was a little more prepared. I had emptied my Dad's ink-jet printing handouts I had designed in Microsoft Word. In the years that followed,

I rarely remember being nervous when speaking to a group, but I recall nerves as I prepped that day.

I grew up in a Bible church, which meant we studied scripture verse-by-verse. Thus, we picked up right where we left off in Ephesians. How strange it felt to have a room full of my friends, listen to what I had to say concerning the Bible. The eclectic group was a surprise. There were people there who I didn't even know identified as Christians. There were also those who I was pretty sure were unbelievers. My scattered thoughts and disjointed words were not much of a lesson, but my peers were attentive. This time I left a little space for discussion at the end. I was surprised by how many different perspectives filled the room.

By the third week, we were packed. No one complained because teens are always looking for excuses to sit close to the opposite sex; bonus if the seating arrangements forced us to squeeze in tight and maybe even touch. Mom and Dad pretty much left us alone when we were in the garage. It was our little haven. Most of the time, we were rockin' out with our 140-decibel band practices. So when something of a quieter nature was happening in our hangout, they didn't pay much attention. They were vaguely aware that I was leading a Bible study but had not even ventured a glance to see how many were attending. Mom and Dad assumed it might be five or six, until one night, as they put it, an eruption of laughter exploded from the direction of the garage. It apparently sounded like a hoard of teens had mysteriously materialized in the attached wing of the house. Dad, in his surprise, crept to the garage window to steal a sneak peek. He was astonished to find what he estimated to be dozens of kids sitting and listening, sometimes laughing at my humorous delivery.

Though he considered all this unexpected, it didn't seem all that odd to me. I was doing it because it meshed a few of the things I loved best. I enjoyed reading my Bible, making my friends laugh, and showing off my drums. So a garage Bible study was the best way to merge my interests.

The group requested that we abandon the verse-by-verse approach and study topics meaningful to high school students. I begrudgingly complied, knowing this would mean more work for me. Over the semester, there were several topics that we covered. We hit the usuals, purity in dating, defending the faith, being bold for God at school—all the subjects familiar to any youth age believer. There was one subject I avoided, though. I never once shared 'the gospel' with the group. I avoided talking about the fundamentals of salvation. I never explained what was required to have eternal life. I avoided it because even then, I was confused. I understood that it had to do with faith in Christ, but I also had become convinced that good works are the proof that one has faith. I could foresee a range of questions on this topic that I didn't know how to answer, so I dodged entirely.

BILLY'S INVITATION

That same year I had an interesting experience while standing outside one of the local Christian rock venues. Billy was a kid who I knew from the marching band. I don't remember him ever attending one of my garage Bible studies, so I'm not sure he knew I was such a Bible nerd. We were both on the drumline together, though he was a couple of years younger than me. We were chatting there in the cool autumn air of an East Texas evening. He and I were there with a group of mutual friends. For some reason, he began to air his doubts about the Christian faith. I had no idea he had any thoughts on Christianity, but it wasn't a surprise to find that his thoughts were negative since Billy was the guy to talk to if you wanted to score some weed.

"So, what happens to all the people in countries where they've never heard about Jesus? God sends them to Hell without giving them a chance? That seems cruel. I'm not so sure about that kind of God."

He wasn't addressing me, but just presenting what he considered a death nail to the group. No one else spoke up, so I stepped forward. I don't remember the answer that I gave him. It probably was a mish-mash of clichés I'd heard from others. It might not even be an answer that I'd be comfortable with today. I was pretty certain that he would return the volley with a more fiery response. I assumed he was looking for a debate. That's why what he said next came as a huge surprise.

"Man, if you were a pastor, I'd be happy to listen to you," he said. I could see sincerity behind those glassy eyes and stoner stare. I was shocked. His question wasn't a 'got-ya.' He was legitimately asking for answers. Somewhere in there among the bong residue and weed smoke, he was thinking it through. I'm sure the conversation went on, but that's where my memory of that night stops.

That comment is even more shocking because it is the only conversation I remember ever having with him. That's because a few months after that, he got drunk and ran his Ford F150 into a tree at about 100 miles per hour. At his funeral, I kept hearing his words ringing again inside my brain cage. He was willing to listen to me on spiritual matters. Could I have helped him? Could I have pulled him toward the light? God gave me the best opportunity, the best opening possible.

This guy had given me an open invitation to talk to him about spiritual subjects. I never took advantage. I don't remember ever inviting him to my Bible study. I never shared the gospel with him. If he was a believer, it wasn't because of me.

My confusion about what was required to gain eternal life did not excuse me from trying to share the gospel, but it was the main reason that I avoided doing so with him. He wasn't the last, though.

A group of friends and I requested permission from the administration of our high school to start a campus Christian club. There was a Christian club for athletes, but we didn't fit in with the Greek physiques in polo shirts. We were of a more artistic bent. The administration explained that every campus club had to have an adult sponsor, and a lunch lady didn't count. After moaning and groaning for a while, we decided to approach our math teacher. It helped that she was my neighbor, and the mom of my friend Todd, the one who had acquainted us with HBO years earlier. When I asked her to sponsor our Christian club, I did not mention that her son had introduced me to porn; it just didn't come up. Within a week, we were set to begin meetings. Meetings would be on Wednesday mornings.

A few dozen of my peers arrived a half hour before school started. We would gather in the math room and talk about issues concerning our faith. It wasn't quite like my garage Bible study since the kids came from a dozen different denominations. It was an open forum discussion that was like the wild west. One moment the charismatics would be talking about that Sunday's miracles while the Baptists squirmed. The next topic would be whether it was ok to make out on a first date. I remember raising a few issues of my own, some embarrassing to mention now.

"Let's talk about how our dollar bills say, 'In God we trust,' while at the same time our country is moving away from God more every day," I said with passion, hoping someone else would climb onto my soapbox with me. Blank stares are all I got. That topic was not as sensational as French kissing.

One thing that marked our discussions was how much we all disagreed on the essentials. Most everyone thought salvation required faith in Jesus, but most would add good works to the equation in some way. We often heard how so-and-so must not be saved since they lived like they were lost.

In thinking back on those years, it is incredibly clear to me now that what my garage Bible study, my friend Billy, and our campus Christian club needed most was a clear explanation of the gospel. We needed it stated and repeated. We needed it written out, spelled out, and shouted out over and over. I had as much opportunity as anyone, and probably more, to share the fundamentals of the gospel with my friends, but I didn't do it. Instead, I decided to talk about the Latin phrases that appear on American legal tender.

Why? Because I couldn't make sense of the fundamentals of the saving message. I was hopelessly confused. Was it faith alone, or did someone have to have good works to be saved? I had heard so many contradicting presentations that there had grown a massive tumor on my desire to share the gospel. I avoided it on multiple occasions because I wasn't sure what to say. I knew that there was something wrong with my understanding of the basics, but I couldn't quite bring it into focus. So instead I talked with believers and unbelievers alike about other topics.

PSEUDO CELEBRITIES

By my junior year in high school, it was becoming clear that there were a lot more gigs for a worship band than a loud rock act. As the worship war was waging in churches, the door was swinging wide for drums and electric guitars where only pipe organs, choirs, and pianos had been before. Much of our energies began to be redirected toward providing the music for youth events and on the odd occasion, even Sunday morning services.

At seventeen years old, I was traveling with a band on the weekends and summers. There seemed to be no shortage of student retreats, D-nows, summer camps, and lock-ins at which we could hawk our worshipful wares. We also sold merchandise such as T-shirts with our worship band's name painted across the chest. Sure, we wanted people to worship God, but we wanted credit for showing them how. Some of these godly gigs we traveled over a thousand miles to play. We hardly made a dime, but it didn't matter. We weekly crawled into my buddies' parent's van and made the long nighttime drives.

As time passed, the gigs grew in size and frequency. Over those years, I produced albums in my garage studio for and traveled with a host of worship and contemporary Christian bands. The names seem funny now. I played with Blue Skies, JumpStart Ministries, Twenty Four Seven, Grace Junkies, Pearl Merchant, and probably a few others I don't remember. We provided wholesome entertainment and worship for thousands of young people across Texas with occasional gigs in Arkansas, Louisiana, Colorado, and Oklahoma.

We were only ever half of the act, though. Every youth event, whether it's a revival, conference, retreat, lock-in, D-now, fifth quarter, or whatever, has at least two parts. The worship band gets the crowd softened up like a lump of kneaded dough. Then the band hands off the dough to the master pastry chef: aka the event speaker, an evangelist style professional talker. He cranks the temperature to maximum and bakes the room until everyone either gets saved or singed in the erratic heat.

A good youth speaker knows how to turn the heat up slowly, though. Since it's student ministry, he'll usually start with a bevy of semi-inappropriate jokes. I remember one such youth evangelist who would open with schtick like, "What do you call a vegan with diarrhea? A salad shooter." He'd follow it with a half dozen poop jokes. After sharing a few laughs with his unsuspecting victims, he'd brilliantly turn the dials as he warmed the crowd.

We once did a gig with a man named Jesse Duplantis. Although we didn't know it until we did the gig, he was a product of the most extreme wing of the prosperity gospel. Duplantis is like the comedian version of Kenneth Copeland. If you can imagine a mix of Robin Williams and Binny Hinn, then you pretty much understand the man. We had no idea what we were getting ourselves into when we agreed to play the event. The gig was arranged by a local community church in Longview, TX. I'm sure they probably shelled out a boatload of cash to bring in such a famous personality. With what funds remained, they booked us, perhaps because we would work for nearly free. Duplantis arrived fashionably late. He took the stage, mic in hand like a night club comedy act. The first words out of that wool wearing wolf were unimaginable.

"This is a three thousand dollar suit," he proclaimed as he popped the collar with his thumb. The audience clapped. I was shocked. He followed that by explaining that he had flown in on his private jet. Apparently, these were the types of blessings that God had in store for the impoverished community of believers who had invited him to speak. I was so appalled, I got up and left the room with a huff. To my knowledge, none of those congregants have received their private jet yet.

He was so clearly a false prophet that we would have refused to do another event with him if the opportunity arose, though others were as manipulative but savvier at hiding their tactics. There was an evangelist named Byron Redburn, who we did a string of events with. Since I'd seen him perform the same talk a dozen times, I was fascinated at how his eyes would fill with tears, and his voice would falter at the same point in the invitational illustration every time. Once while doing an event at a summer camp in Arkansas, he was ambushed by a group of angry youth ministers. They accused him of emotionally manipulating their students with tears and stories of the untimely deaths of young people. Their primary accusation was that he was crying on cue. In retrospect, I think the offended youth ministers were most likely right.

At an event in East Texas, a particularly effective speaker named Max Lynch explained to the assembled students that they needed to think of their lives as a piece of pottery. They were then to turn this life-jar upside down and empty it. Then they were to allow God to fill the jar with those things He desired. This experience was supposed to come with utter emotional brokenness. Tears and sobbing were expected. An hour after the session, I found myself down by the lake staring over the water, asking God's help to empty my life. I squinted, I grimaced, I might have even pinched myself, but the tears didn't come.

Loads of buzz words were used to whip the kids up into a frenzy at these kinds of events. Brokenness, surrender, reckless abandon, rededication, deliverance, and many more were all favorite catchphrases of these emotional manipulators. Carefully crafted invitations were designed to bring the attendees to their knees and tears.

I have a youth minister friend who told me recently that he was planning a camp for his youth. The speaker he was thinking of using for the event braggingly said, "Do you want me to make them cry? I can make them cry."

"Why would I want them to cry?" My friend asked, sincerely. "That's a weird thing to want." The oddness of it never occurred to me in the years I was involved in that style of ministry. The more tears shed at a youth retreat, the more the so-called presence of God had arrived. The more crying experienced at a youth camp, the more lives that were supposedly changed for the better.

That was the mentality and the method: Make them cry, and they will surrender their lives to Jesus. In principle, I bought into the bully tactics. I even played my part. With what little information that I had, it seemed to work for everyone else. However, there was a fundamental problem for me.

I could never drum up the kind of emotion that I saw others experiencing. I was too honest to pretend to be having some esoteric extravaganza when I wasn't. I was too emotionally insulated to give myself over to such flights of exotic fanaticism. I was privy to too many emotionally driven events to be moved by the resplendent display of enthusiasm and sentimentalism. I was stuck between my desire to participate in the emotional demonstration, and my inability to experience anything like what we were being pressured to feel.

There was this halo placed around emotion. Week after week, event after event, we were being told that saved people feel big emotions about God, Christ, and the cross. We were being led to believe that those with eternal life would inevitably experience perpetual gratitude for salvation, inexpressible affection for God, and everlasting ecstasy at being His child. The inverse message was unstated but clear enough. Those who felt no emotion probably weren't saved.

I heard statements like this more than once. "If you can't feel the presence of the living God in this place, you might be spiritually dead." This kind of statement was also commonly repeated: "If you don't feel brokenness about your sin, then you need to carefully consider whether you're really a Christian."

The solution for most people who attended these kinds of events was simple. Show some emotion. A tear would do the trick. Getting down on one's knees is even better. Weeping aloud is the gold standard.

I remember so many times, sitting in the back of the dimly lit room wishing I could participate. I longed to feel what everyone else seemed to be feeling. I often wondered what was wrong with me. On some rare occasions, I even entertained the notion that I wasn't saved.

Since I was a ministry insider, playing drums on the worship band, I got to spend a lot of back-stage time with these speakers and evangelists. I expected sincerity and earnestness from these men of ministry. Although some exhibited piety even in the green-room, what I saw as often as not was cynicism and irreverence. The perpetual emotionalism that they invited their audience into was not the way they themselves lived.

This discovery was like finding out that Superman uses his x-ray vision to look up women's skirts. The pedestal I had put these effective evangelists on wobbled and tumbled to the ground. These pseudo-celebrities of the youth event circuit were not immoral or sinful; necessarily, they didn't demonstrate the kind of emotionalism they prescribed. Two options lay ahead for me. I could buy into the mysticism of Christian sentimentality, or I could become like them, cynical.

In those years, my wide-eyed naiveté was converted

into cold hard cynicism. I refashioned myself in the image of these emotional manipulators, hardly ever believing in the drug I prescribed. I continued to play my part in these effusive events but became more doubtful about their effectiveness as time went on.

I sincerely loved Jesus. I genuinely wanted others to love Him as well, but I was losing hope in the only method I knew to accomplish the task. Church and event ministry had lost its glow, and it left me feeling empty and disappointed. It was a confusing time. It made me step back and reconsider all I knew about how we talk to people about the gospel. I wasn't aware of any alternative, but it left me wondering why we spoke of the gospel at all since so much of it seemed to be a false performance.

STAN'S HAND OFF

I got my first church job at the age of 19. I was hired on as the pastoral intern at a small Bible church. I was the first one the church had ever had. It wasn't clear what the job description was. I met with the pastor a few times a week. The majority of our time was given to reading aloud. I know it sounds strange, but... no, it was strange, now that I think about it. I don't remember the name of the book, but the cover was orange, and it was a biography on a revival preacher from the 1700s named Jonathan Edwards. I cared nothing about what we were reading. The pastor sipped day-old coffee by the styrofoam cup load as I read page after page.

One thing I do remember about Jonathan Edwards was that he had his first pastoral job when he was only 18 years old. A stab of pain could be felt on that one. I was already 19, and only a pastor's audiobook. I did not feel useful in that internship and looked forward to the day that it would end. As a result of that experience, I unequivocally decided that I would not ever be an intern at a church again.

So, my next job was intern for the youth group of a church across town. I know, my commitment to stay away from church work was laughable. I had landed the job at *the* big Baptist church. It had it all: steeple, pipe organ, and a clearly written job description for interns. I had been in the Bible church all my life, but I learned quickly that the Baptists paid better. Not-to-mention, being a youth intern, was a lot more fun, mainly because it didn't involve being a book on tape.

As the college-age summer intern for the Baptist youth group, I led game time, helped plan events, and occasionally taught the Bible lesson. The Baptist church was less concerned with biblical acuity, and I appreciated the lack of scrutiny. As an intern, I was allowed to *share from the heart*, which is *a license not to prepare*. It was easy, and I breezed through those short hot months with the greatest of enjoyment.

The youth minister, Stan, was in his late twenties. He had been raised as a constantly sun tanned California kid before his parents moved to Texas. I always thought of him as a healthy mix of surfer, radio DJ, and a friendly young uncle. He could coax a load of laughs out of any room, whether by means appropriate or otherwise. His youth ministry was a haven from the stuffy rules and drama of teenage life for about a hundred and fifty town kids.

Stan taught me a lot about serving youth. My time in his office was very different than my first internship at the Bible church. We talked about life and love and ministry. He got a thrill out of seeing young people, including me, growing and making good life decisions. Being in the Bible church all my life, I had grown up thinking there was nothing of value in any other church in town. Now I was beginning to see that there was an entire ecosystem of believers that was not only alive but thriving. Working with Stan at the Baptist church was like realizing I could breathe underwater and discovering a whole new world below the surface.

One of our main events each year was summer camp. The youth group was big enough to do our own camp, but the year I came on board, Stan decided to register the kids at a more traditional small-town summer camp. He did this with a note of intention since he would soon be shouldering a new responsibility. We invested a lot of time and money into planning for that oh-so-important week. It was to be a five day stint of high octane activity finely calibrated to evoke an emoti-spiritual response from the kids.

The week came with a burgeoning concern. Stan, the energetic leader of this camp bound conglomerate, had one lingering inconvenient family obligation. He had a spousal priority, which threatened to upset the delicate balance between the youth group and leader. I suppose it was not entirely unexpected, but Stan's wife called on the second day of camp and informed him he needed to come home immediately. She was about to give birth to their twins. Obviously, his priorities were upside down because he totally fell for it, leaving his youth group in the hands of an intern.

"Ok, you're in charge." He said as he fumbled with his keys. He and his wife were having their first children, and he was overjoyed. "I love you, man." He said in a rare moment of sincerity. I repeated the same as he climbed into his car. I'd never told him or any other man such a thing, but I had that warm brotherly love that comes from working and achieving together.

I remember the strange feeling as I watched Stan's truck drive out of the camp gate, dust billowing up from the back tires. In reality, there was hardly anything different. Stan, in his wisdom, had chosen this camp because it basically ran itself. I was a glorified babysitter for the rest of the week, but it was a fantastic feeling to be the one trusted with such an important ministry. The three remaining days went off without a single injury, death, or teen pregnancy. It felt good to be needed and trusted and as we drove back, I knew I had found a line of work that I wouldn't soon part with.

It was much better than reading aloud a dusty old book about a dead dude from the 1700s. The work felt relevant and meaningful. The Baptist church held a real sense of excitement. Every week there was another adventure. Those months raced by with unending novelty.

My youth internship ended with the summer, and I continued with my college education. In addition to all this, I was still doing weekend gigs with my band, which often left me drowsy for class. I was studying Bible, history/political science, and psychology. It was the cocktail approach to seeking a university diploma. They called it an interdisciplinary degree. I called it 'the path of least resistance.' It turns out there are quite a lot of books about dead guys from the 1700s along the way to a diploma, though I could never get anyone to read them aloud to me.

One afternoon I got a call from Stan, the youth minister. It had been many years since I'd spent any time with him. He talked to me, not as an intern, but as an old friend. "Why don't you come by the church this Wednesday night. I want to talk to you about something," he said, not giving a hint to what was on his mind. I agreed readily looking forward to visiting my old haunt.

Entering the building and climbing the flights of stairs to arrive at the youth room was a blast from before. The blue carpet, raised stage, and the third-floor view of downtown brought all the memories from that fantastic summer rushing back. I could feel the nostalgia as the smell of the room hit my nose. I walked in as I had done countless times before. Stan was still hard at work. It was as if time had stood still since I had left. He was as energetic as ever. As he wrapped up Bible study, I plopped down in the back.

"How would you like to be the youth minister here?" he asked after the meeting. The kids were gone by now.

"What?" I stammered. "Seriously?" I contained myself, but inwardly I was leaping at the surprise opportunity like a starved street dog. In the years since I had seen Stan, I had worked as the youth director of a tiny church that smelled like mildew and was an hour's drive away from my house. I enjoyed my time there but wished for a position less smelly and closer to home. I wouldn't get closer to home than this, and the smell of the building held a bouquet of warm memories.

"That'd be cool," I croaked out sheepishly, trying not to overplay my excitement. "Are you leaving?" I asked, trying not to think only of my own machinations.

"Yeah, I've been offered a position at a church in another town." I congratulated him as we talked about what he would be doing at his new church. I restrained myself from saying, "Enough about you, now let's talk about me!"

In due course, Stan walked me down to his office, soon to be my office, and we continued the conversation. The church would form a search committee, but I was to be the interim minister of students. Stan explained that I would be considered for the position if I chose to throw my name in the hat.

"Why me?" I managed to ask as we chatted.

"Remember that time at camp?" he asked as his lips curled upward into a smile.

"Yeah."

"You were only 19, but I knew I could trust you with 150 kids for a week." I stared at the carpet, trying not to show my gleaming pride. "This is kind of like that."

"What do you mean?" I asked, not quite seeing the connection.

"I've worked hard to get this ministry where it is. I want to hand it off to someone who I can trust to carry on, keep it strong, and continue the work."

He loved the kids. He loved the town. I could tell with those words that it was hard letting go. He would soon drive out of town, once again as I stayed behind to do my best at shepherding the flock he had gathered. I was so excited to be part of something important. Within a week, the keys to the building were in my hand.

TWELVE
SALVATIONS

Being in the Baptist sphere came with its own idiosyncrasies. One such awkwardness was what was known as the *invitation.* Growing up in the Bible church meant that I had not been introduced to the end of service time, where individuals are encouraged to walk down the aisle as a means to solidify salvation. A given Sunday's sermon could be on the topic of vanity in Ecclesiastes, romance in the Song of Solomon, or the children of Israel crossing the Red Sea. No matter. At the end of any sermon on any topic, the compliant Baptist preacher was duty-bound to abandon his topic and give a gospel presentation replete with a sinner's prayer and a call to "come down front." All this was done as the familiar pipe organ melody of *Jesus is waiting* played softly through the lofty rafters. It seemed to me that Jesus spent a lot of time waiting because most Sundays, no one traversed the velvet carpet.

I was the square peg in this round hole system. I quietly resisted this traditional practice, not feeling that it had a clear basis in Scripture. When I was a guest speaker at various churches, which happened a lot in those days, I would pull the local minister aside and ask if he would do the invitation. I never gave my true reason for wanting to avoid calling people to the front. "As a guest speaker," I would explain, "I don't know your congregation as well as you do. At the end of the sermon, I'll pass you the mic, and you can give the invitation."

This approach probably seemed quite strange to many a pastor who invited me to speak, but it was my half-hearted attempt to stay true to my wavering convictions. It only represented part of my concerns. In reality, I didn't have any faith in the aisle. I was certain that something was amiss with the entire affair, but I could not quite grasp the problem. In addition to this, I had heard so many different contradictory invitationals, that it seemed the actual content was not important. It didn't seem to matter what the preacher said during the invitation as long as he got butts out of pews and down front. The number would be divided into *salvations* and *rededications,* recorded and cataloged as if it were an actual victory. Though for me, it never felt like an uptick in the scoreboard. It felt like those who had moved to the front were hardly ever changed by the journey to the altar.

The most audacious reason that I resisted doing an altar call was because I wasn't sure what it should include. Some preachers pressured parishioners to promise their lives to Christ publicly. Others included a faith alone approach, which always seemed to contradict the need to walk down the aisle. Other pulpit bangers claimed that their listeners needed to repent of their sins and get their lives right. I simply was not sure what "version" I should invite people into. It seemed that with every invitation I heard the gospel was blurring further out of focus. The growing fuzziness drove me to avoid ever giving an altar call.

In my capacity as interim student minister at the big Baptist church, I tried my best to hide my aversion to the invitation. At first, it was easy enough, but I had to get more and more creative as I went along. A Baptist who doesn't do an invitation is like a fish that doesn't swim. I was able to avoid performing an invitation for nearly six months before the whole thing unraveled. It wasn't the deacons or the pastor who finally pressured me into the uncomfortable practice. The impetus came from an unexpected place.

Stan had left me a healthy youth group that was ripe for even more growth. I had focused on creating an inviting environment for kids to come and spend time together. We had a great student worship band. They took the reigns and weekly gave their time to improvement. In short, they rocked, but they would soon gain a member that would take them to the next plane of existence.

I remember the day that Tommy showed up. He was a solid six and a half foot man. At least he looked it, though he was only seventeen. "Where do I set up?" He said in a deeply mature voice as he walked through the door with his Jackson electric guitar and Orange amp in tow. I was stunned by the sheer size of the guy. "I'm playing with the band tonight," he informed me. I'm not sure if he had been invited to do so, but if he had, the invitation didn't come from me. I quickly surveyed him, noting that he was wearing chains thick enough to tow a car, and jeans so baggy he could hide an arsenal of weapons. He was not legally old enough to have them, but his arms were covered in tattoos. No doubt, he had easily convinced the frightened tattoo artist that he was of proper age. Not wanting to get beat up by a "youth," I pointed him to the stage, and he began to set up his rig.

The "kid" could shred. I'm not sure that what he added was exactly worshipful, but it was impressive. He stood head and shoulders above the rest of the band, and his massive size made his guitar look like a toy in his gorilla-sized hands. The band from then on played a little louder, faster, and more aggressively.

He quickly became a regular attendee. I'm sure it was no coincidence that the female population of the youth group began to grow exponentially. The rock n' worship band melted faces with ripping solos, and melted hearts with soaring ballads. Tommy was quick becoming an inadvertent leader in the youth group, though he didn't seem to know it. He had a fan club of about a dozen girls who were at least his age, but half his height. They seemed to be ever in orbit of him with spacey looks in their star-filled eyes. I'm sure, had their daddies known the look of the situation; they would have come after me with torches and pitchforks. Tommy was the church's *bad boy* and the good girls, who had seen only soft palmed emo-kids were smitten.

It was a hot Wednesday night as the students poured into the youth room. The summer was beginning, and there was a growing buzz for our packed schedule. We did two goofy games, the band played three ear-splitting songs, and now it was my time to get up and teach. I had prepared to talk from 2 Corinthians. For some reason, I had decided I didn't need to mark my Bible. Instead, I was planning to simply open to the right passage and preach to the kids. I thumbed through my pages. The passage I landed on was not in second Corinthians but in first. I don't know why I did this, but instead of fumbling to find the right passage, which I had prepared, I simply preached from the verses that my Bible fell open to. They were not at all related to what I had planned, and I'm not sure what I talked about. It seemed to me that the kids didn't know any different.

As I wrapped up my half-hour of babbling about who knows what, I was about to dismiss the students. It was my practice to turn them out without any kind of invitational, aisle walking, or altar call. As I was about to say, "see you guys next week," Tommy took action.

I watched him rise from his seat like a bottle rocket. All six and a half feet shot up from the back row. His rock star groupies all looked up at him, as surprised as I was. I thought *this is it. He's finally going to do it; he'll murder us all.* Before he spoke, my heart was already beating fast. I looked into his eyes from across the room, and I could see that he was adamant. I steeled myself for trouble.

"What are we supposed to do to get saved?" He said almost as if he was mad. "Whatever it is, I don't want us to leave until we've all done it." He stood there monolithic like a mountain of stone. This would be my downfall. It was like he could see through me. Everyone else was too soft to admit that I had been avoiding the obvious. He, however, was more of a man than me. He was demanding that I share the plan of salvation, and it looked as if he'd physically block the way if I didn't give up the ancient secret.

Taking a step forward, he added, "If we need to come down front or pray a prayer, or whatever, then let's do it. I'm tired of not knowing what will happen to me when I die."

A long beat followed as I tried to figure out what to

do. I had never been pressured by the pastor, or the deacons, or any of the other staff. I had never been told to do an altar call, but now I was backed into a corner by this giant kid. I quickly rambled through my memories, trying to decide how to proceed.

"Yeah, good point Tommy," I began. "I'll... or I mean... yeah." I bumbled for a few seconds as he stood waiting, staring, maybe brooding. "Ok," I said. It seemed to me that most preachers had people close their eyes. "Let's close our eyes." Heads all over the room bowed and eyes closed. It felt good to get everyone's eyes off of me. I took a deep breath. Now what? Usually, an altar call included music, but that wouldn't work because the guitar player was determined to get saved, so...

"Repeat after me," I said. It wasn't as if I had never heard an altar call before. I knew what others were doing. I knew the industry standard. My conscience was screaming, "don't do it; you know it's not in the Bible!" *But I have to,* I thought. *What a weird form of persecution.* I was in danger of getting martyred if I refused to share the plan of salvation. Reluctantly I gave in and surrendered the last vestige of resistance I had.

Step one: have them repeat the sinner's prayer. I felt weird doing it, but I was too much of a coward to do anything else. Step two: ask who prayed the prayer for the first time being careful to have them raise their hands only while everyone's eyes are still closed. I was ashamed as I looked out across the crowd, counting silently to myself. No less than twelve hands, including Tommy's raised higher than all the rest, shot upward. Step three: have them come to the front as a "public profession of faith." All twelve did.

I clapped along with the rest of the youth group, but the celebratory racket was a den to me. Outwardly I congratulated them, but inside it didn't feel right. I didn't doubt the sincerity of the moment. In fact, I didn't doubt that this was a very important experience for them. Ultimately, what I doubted was myself. I wasn't sure that I hadn't just led them astray. What I had been trying to avoid for six months had placed itself squarely in my path, and I was too weak to go around. I was being transformed into something that I wasn't comfortable with.

In the following weeks, I was hailed as an evangelist. I was celebrated as a life changer. The so-called twelve salvations were announced the following Sunday. Though, the jubilant applause came with an ever echoing emptiness for me. This was not least because it wasn't long before Tommy stopped coming. The fan club, twelve strong who just happened to be the same ones who answered the altar call that night, soon dropped off as well. Out of that twelve, four began a small group Bible study which met for two weeks, and then it too dissolved. Within three months of that peculiar night, I had nothing to show for the twelve salvations which I had supposedly won. Though those twelve salvations were written down in the Church registry, I couldn't say for sure whether anyone had gotten saved. Something wasn't right, and I didn't know how to fix it. I honestly didn't know if we had twelve salvations, a dozen rededications, or nothing at all.

ROAD TRIP

From the time I was sixteen, I have been driving very used cars. My first was a Nissan Pulsar. I often told people, "The great thing about this car is that when something breaks, the broken part usually falls off on the road, so I don't have to worry about it." My next car was a hand-me-down; my older brother had thoroughly abused it by the time I was able to take it for a spin. My third vehicle was one that I was proud of, though it still had the wear of age.

I saw an ad for a used Jeep in the newspaper. Yeah, that's right: it was still the best way to find used cars. An older guy was selling a cherry red Cherokee, and the moment I saw it, I knew it was for me. He wanted four thousand dollars for this beauty. I thought four G's was a pretty good price for a twenty-year-old vehicle. It was the first car I could take a girl on a date in and not feel like a total junkyard baboon.

The main thing I was excited about was—and I cannot stress this enough—the back seat laid down.

That was important to me because I loved camping. I adored the idea of having solo wilderness adventures. I'd arrive like the rugged mountain man I am, throw my sleeping bag in the back of the Jeep, and slumber to the melodic sounds of the chilly forest night.

I handed over the dough, and the red adventure wagon was mine. That left me strapped for cash, but I was determined to take my Jeep on its maiden voyage before the summer was in full swing. I marked out six days that I could get away, which was not easy considering my schedule at the church. I had $114 to make the entire round trip. It would be a Ramen noodle kind of journey, but I knew how to live on meager rations. I had a solid plan with a handful of stops.

It had been a while since I visited my friends in Cameron, Texas. I decided to make this one of my destinations. I didn't account for the fact that these friends had jobs and lived in the middle of nowhere. They owned about a dozen noisy dogs. Without much of a plan, I took off for their ranch. I arrived as the rain started. It rained the entire time I was there. I was stuck in a house with a bunch of pent up dogs for days while their owners were away at work. I didn't need much more motivation than that to move on. Indeed, that was not yet the manly adventure for which I had been searching. From there, I headed northeast.

The Davy Crocket National Forest is an excellent place to camp, as long as you like humidity so thick you can fill your water bottle with it, mosquitoes so big that their bite should constitute a blood transfusion, and nighttime temperatures that dip down into the low 100s. I had imagined the fantastic adventure I'd have there. Within an hour of my arrival, I wished it was raining again.

It was so hot I couldn't stand to make a fire. The chill of the cold hot dog weenie was my only comfort. One other family was occupying a campsite, and they had a climate-controlled trailer. The low hum of their air conditioner unit was the only sound I could hear as I paced around the stifling forest. As the sun beamed its dappled light through the tall pines, I expected the afternoon to give way to cooler evening temperatures. Unfortunately, the blanket of sappy pine needles overhead worked with the humidity to keep the evening temperature at the same convection scorch.

The gnawing boredom was equally excruciating. Why had I wanted this to be a solo trip? If I had had someone with me, I could have at least shared my discontent with another human. Only the trees could hear my frustrated grumbles here. I walked around the loop of trails a half dozen times, sweat dripping down and soaking my clothes. Never had I seen a campground without a body of water. I expected a lake, a river, a stream, or even a water fountain. Even in the toilets, there was no running water. The attraction of this campsite was that it had pines, pines, and more pines. I had seen pine trees all my life and was in no need of more.

As the evening turned to night, I took contemplative comfort in the fact that I would soon stretch out in the luxurious back of my new Jeep Cherokee. I lay down the seat and stretched a t-shirt over the open window to keep out bugs but release the heat in the car. I chucked my sleeping bag in the back and crawled in. I was horrified at what I found.

No, it wasn't a rattlesnake or a black widow. I found that the back of the Jeep was not long enough for me to lie down. In my excitement to buy this adventure wagon, I had not measured its back compartment. What I had assumed would be a comfortable bed was a cramped, too-short, claustrophobia-inducing coffin. I had made a point never to use profanity, but this was a time that some could have come in handy. The best I could do was to spread out in a diagonal arrangement. The back door left a divot in my skull and a crick in my neck as my feet jammed uncomfortably between the bucket seats, though it was soon apparent that I had a bigger problem.

The only bedding I had with me was an expensive, thick, cold-weather sleeping bag from my Boy Scout days. The tag boasted that you could stay warm in temperatures as low as zero degrees. That had been an essential feature on the hiking trips that took us, ranging over the chilly Ozark mountains. On a scorching night in the back of an already hot Jeep, simply laying on top of the bag could spontaneously ignite my epidermis.

As I lay there fuming in more ways than one, I began to ask myself, "What in the world am I doing out here?" I couldn't afford to run the car's air conditioner all night. I'd probably wake up to an empty tank and have to spend the rest of my life in these blazing woods. I was mad at everything. However, I tried my best to sleep through the night, but at midnight, I couldn't take it any longer.

In the middle of the night, I made an executive decision. I did a quick mental calculation as I cranked the car. The next stop on my road trip was supposed to be a few hours drive. I didn't want to arrive too early, knowing that the person I was going to visit wouldn't be up until a reasonable hour. So I determined that if I drove about fifteen miles an hour, I could turn a two-hour trip into a six-hour odyssey. That would allow me to arrive at an appropriate morning hour.

The heat must have baked my brain because even as I say this, I realize that it's a stupid idea. Stupid or not, though, that's what I did. I crawled through a middle swath of South Texas at a snail's pace through the wee hours of the morning. I wasn't too afraid of falling asleep since no one had ever died from a 15-mile-an-hour impact, as far as I knew. A scene from an old Chris Farley movie was on repeat in my mind. It's the one where he gets stopped for driving seven miles an hour. After making a two-hour drive in a little over six hours, I pulled into the town where I had been heading.

The most memorable visit of that trip was the one I paid my brother in Nacogdoches. He had moved there to go to the big state school in our area. We were still in that awkward phase that all brothers must go through. The friendship of childhood had been mandatory, but now we were figuring out how adult brothers of college-age transition into a voluntary relationship. I thought the trip would be a good step toward bridging the gap from boyhood to being adult friends.

I was tired of driving as I pulled onto his street. I had never seen his place before and I was a little intimidated. The brownish exterior bore the marks of an underwhelming maintenance crew and what little grass remained on the balding lawn showed signs of neglect. That was the kind of affordable living that dots the real estate surrounding any large university. The relative squalor of college life was not something I had yet grown accustomed to. I pulled to a stop in front of his apartment and started trepidatious toward his door.

"Hey, want a beer?" he said as the door swung wide. I declined, having not ever tasted the stuff. I was quite determined not to try a mind-altering chemical for the first time in an unfamiliar place. His roommates were milling about. Everyone seemed to have a beer can glued to their hand. Like automatic weapon cartridges, they shot, discarded, and reloaded with impressive regularity.

At least the place had an air conditioner, which was an improvement on the Jeep coffin. I was going to sleep on the couch that evening. As the day turned to night, we flew by my usual bedtime at an alarming speed. These vampires lived a more nocturnal life than I did. At some point in the evening, my brother's roommate spilled a full can of beer on the couch, or I suppose I should say, on my bed. Suddenly the back of my Jeep didn't seem so bad.

As I sank lower and lower into the Coors-scented couch, trying to claim more cushioned real estate, the guys talked about their party lifestyle. I had known that my brother was living a different kind of life than the one I had chosen, but this was the first time I had come face to face with the gritty reality. The stories they shared were an irreverent homage to college living. I felt troubled by the discussion as I drifted off.

On the next morning, I rose and was ready to get on the road. I was supposed to make it to College Station to visit another friend there. I was up before the party animals and was going to slip out quietly. I walked out of the front doorway. I was relieved to be leaving but I was shocked at what I saw. I stared at the parking lot for a long moment. Had I been drinking after all? Confused and upset, I marched back into the apartment.

"Hey," I said, as I banged on my brother's bedroom

door, "My car is gone!"

"What do you mean?" a voice said from behind me. Despite his late night, he was up at this relatively early hour making coffee. He had an impressive tolerance for absorbing vast amounts of nighttime alcohol and then rising early for his morning work schedule.

"I parked in front of your apartment last night. Now my Jeep is gone. Have you guys had any cars stolen from here? If someone has stolen my car..." He interrupted.

"It got towed," he said as he casually gulped the coffee he had just made. "You have to have a parking pass. They're strict about towing."

"Why didn't you tell me?" I asked though I suspected it was because he had been pretty busy getting inebriated the night before. I tried to keep myself calm.

"Well, there used to be a 'you will get towed' sign. My buddy got drunk and ran over it the other day." I thought I noted a slight smile on that one. I wasn't really in the mood.

"So, where's my car now?" I said, wanting the entire episode to be over.

"I don't know. I guess you could ask at the office. They would know where the impound is." At his words, I walked out the door and began heading for the office. Before I got across the unkempt lawn, I realized something. I turned once more and stuck my head in the door.

"Do you have work today?" I said.

"Yep, I'm about to leave."

"Ok. I'm going to need a ride— somewhere," I said as I shut the door a little too hard. Our adult friendship was getting off to a great start.

It cost me $150 to get my Jeep out of the impound. That meant I had to make a trip to the ATM. Adding to my $114, I had to use my ATM card as credit and intentionally overdrew my account to cover the cost. I knew I was going to get a penalty for it, but at this point, I didn't want any more "help" from my brother, I just wanted to go home.

Though the entire experience was a pitiful one, there was one aspect that echoed around in my head as I drove back north. In fact over the following years, I wrestled with this dubious doubt. I knew my brother had become a believer at a young age. I was there when it happened. I remembered the moment in that bunk bed when Dad shared the gospel. Now, he was deliberately living an ungodly lifestyle. What did that mean? There was a preacher I knew who would say things like, "If you're really saved, you can't deliberately live in sin." Was it possible that my brother was not *really* saved? The notion put a knot in my stomach and left me with all kinds of jagged uncomfortable emotions. By that definition, and I wasn't sure if it was right, my brother was going to Hell.

MY ROLE

The year I served as the interim youth minister was the busiest of my life. The summer was especially hectic. I made my first two international mission trips. I led the student ministry through a packed summer schedule and I played at a handful of summer camps with my band.

My band did a two-week camp in Arkadelphia, Arkansas. It was our first "big gig." There were hundreds of students from dozens of churches. They had come from four different states. The camp, which was called *Reach*, was an essential step in the life of the group. That was mostly because of one man. The speaker for that week was a well known evangelist named Jon Randles. He was a brilliant speaker who could hold the attention of any crowd. He was funny, but on a dime, he would turn and say the most poignant things. The guy enamored me.

I was sad to see our two-week stint come to an end, primarily because I had so enjoyed listening to Jon. As I went back to my home town and returned to the youth ministry, I imagined becoming a speaker like him. There was something about his words that were clear and compelling. He didn't burden his listeners with a boatload of confusing phrases, as so many Baptist evangelists and speakers often did. His gospel approach was simple and understandable. This guy was different, almost an enigma to me. I only wished I could get some more time with him.

A few weeks later, my bandmates and I got a call from our lead singer. She wanted to have a band meeting. That was uncommon. We didn't ever have meaningless meetings; we had always used our time together to practice. It was clear that something out of the ordinary was in play.

"Jon Randles called me," she said. Laney was not only a great worship leader and singer but a fantastic band manager. She was virtually beaming as she relayed the conversation. "He's invited us to be the worship band for Paradigm." One of the band member's jaw fell open. He knew what that meant. The rest of us were in the dark. She explained.

"Paradigm is one of the biggest college worship services in the state. It happens every week in Lubbock, Texas, near the campus of Texas Tech. There are anywhere from a thousand to fifteen hundred students there every week." she said exuberantly. We had never been too concerned by the size of the crowd. Years earlier, we had started the band for a local college Bible study, which had an attendance of eight, six of which were in the band. "They want us to come this fall."

As we talked, I could hardly believe what I was hearing. It was the chance of a lifetime. It wasn't the size of the audience that I was most excited about, though. It was the fact, as I found out, that Jon Randles was the weekly speaker for Paradigm. I would get the chance to not only listen to his teaching but to build a personal relationship with the guy. We buzzed electrically for the next months as the time approached.

There were some complications to work out. Namely, Lubbock was an eight-hour drive away. I was in my Junior year of college, and my tuition was free. I knew it would be irresponsible to drop out, so I began to scheme a way to stay at the university I was at and get to Lubbock once a week. In addition to this, I was still the student ministry director in my home town. It was a puzzle to imagine how this semester was going to come together.

Only a college kid would entertain the idea of trying to balance such a ridiculous number of obligations. Monday through Wednesday, I was in class at my University in Longview. Sundays and Wednesday nights, I was leading youth meetings. Thursday morning, I would drive to Dallas and get on a jet headed for Lubbock. Thursday night, I'd play with the band. We'd hit the sack late, rise early to hop on another plane headed home. I'd return in time for Friday afternoon class at the university. Saturday, I'd prepare for Sunday youth meeting. Then the week would begin again. I was also on the rotation to lead worship for chapel at my university, and I hosted the campus comedy show that semester as well. Each of these obligations required more preparation time than I was able to give them.

Nonetheless, they got done. Somewhere in there, I had to fit study, sleep, and occasionally eating. Oh, and did I mention that I had a girlfriend at the time. I'm sure we saw each other during the week, but I was a pretty absent and absent-minded boyfriend.

What I loved most about the manic schedule was the fact that I got to spend an evening with Jon Randles. He, too, had a busy schedule, busier than mine by far. He would often drive in from a revival, or speaking engagement just in time. We'd sit down for a half-hour or so before Paradigm and catch up. After the worship service, we'd usually hit a local all-night burger shop and sit around and chat for an hour or so. He was different than the other "professional" speakers I'd met. He had managed to stay untouched by the usual cynicism that had gripped most of the traveling evangelists I knew.

I asked Jon to mentor me. He was happy to have an apprentice and gladly invited me to join him on the road. My schedule didn't allow many trips, but when he was in the region, I'd hop in with him and ride along. It seemed that ninety percent of his job was to drive to the next event. Along the long stretches of west Texas roads, we'd talk about the nuts and bolts of doing the kind of ministry he did. I saw it as a certain kind of magic, and I wanted to learn the tricks of the trade. He had mastered life on the road, and he was the best I had ever seen at what he did.

After one of those long drives, we arrived at a little church which he was to speak at for an evening revival. We had driven three hours to get there. He hopped out of the car and began rifling through the trunk like a raccoon. "What are you looking for?" I asked.

"A Bible," He said casually.

"You don't have a Bible you preach out of?" I asked, surprised.

"I don't need the Bible for me; I need it for them," he said with that familiar smile.

"What do you mean?" I asked.

"I have all the verses I'll preach memorized, but West Texas Baptists carry guns, and they'll use em' on me if I go up there to preach without a Bible in my hand." He went back to rummaging as we laughed. After a moment, he found that for which he was searching. He produced a camouflage covered Gideon sized Bible. "You think that'll work?" he asked as he tucked it into his back pocket. We laughed as we headed toward the church now only a few minutes late.

"I was preaching for a youth revival in Dallas. Afterward, a guy came up really confused," Jon said as we came to the door. He paused with his hand on the handle. He wanted to finish his story before we entered the building. "The guy said, 'are you dyslexic? I told him, 'no.' He said, 'Oh, I was just wondering cause you preached that entire sermon with your Bible upside down.'" We entered the building, giggling like a couple of kids.

It wasn't just that he was fun to be around. In the year I spent getting to know Jon, I noticed something about his teaching that was strangely missing from most other evangelists. He made a sharp distinction between salvation and discipleship. He had this fun phrase that he would use to talk about the moment someone gets saved. He would say, "Once you step through the Stargate, you can never go back. It's done. It's taken care of." I liked this primarily because I was a huge sci-fi fan, and Stargate was one of my favorite movies. He would explain salvation as a one-time event. Many people were living as *"Casual Christians."* Most of his time was spent trying to get people who were saved to begin to live as *"Dangerous Disciples."*

He acknowledged that there were believers who were saved who didn't take the next step of discipleship. That was new to me, but even at the time, I didn't soak it up. I didn't grasp the monumental difference in what he was saying. The terms had become so muddled to me that salvation and discipleship seemed to be essentially the same thing. It's only in retrospect that I look back and realize the seeds that he had planted in my mind and heart. These seeds would not bloom for years to come. It wouldn't be until they were watered by an unexpected source that I would finally come to understand what Jon Randles was talking about.

Toward the end of that hectic semester, I was beginning to feel the effects of that crazy schedule. I could tell I needed some time to think and, more importantly, sleep. I had turned in all my work for my classes at the university. Soon I would move to Lubbock to play with the band.

I was sitting in my office at the church one Monday morning. The fall semester of Paradigm had ended, and I was approaching a much-needed winter break. It was as if I could feel the speed of it all slowing to a normative pace. I hadn't had time to simply sit and think, something that I used to do all the time. I loved taking an hour here and there in a comfortable chair to ponder the new things I'd learned. Throughout my life, this was one of my favorite practices. I would often find a piano on campus where I'd casually adlib on the keys as I thought through my day. I hadn't had time to process all that happened and all I'd learned.

I was looking out the window leaning back in my oversized office chair. My mind was wandering over the many things I had heard from Jon Randles and the dozens of other evangelists we'd work with in the previous years. I was comparing all that against the Bible lessons I'd been teaching my students at the church. It was hardly a Freudian slip, but out of my mouth came these words—"What is my role in my salvation?"

It was a passing thought ambling by. I didn't consider it a sign of a problem at the time. These were the kinds of things that I would sit around and ponder. In looking back, however, that simple phrase completely encapsulated the fullness of my confusion. I was reasonably confident that Jesus had saved me, but I wasn't sure what I had done to gain that salvation. In fact, I wasn't even sure if I was currently doing something that allowed me to maintain my salvation. Jon Randles' words became another ingredient in the theological stew that boiled in my mind. I was struggling to understand what allowed someone to be saved. I wanted, no needed, to understand.

BEAT IT

There is always a war of technology going on in media. For reasons I will explain in a moment, the industry chose 8mm cameras and projectors over other technology. When I was young, the battle was between VHS and Betamax. Beta was superior in image quality. However, VHS won the battle and became the household standard for recording and watching movies. Tape rental houses popped up, shelves lined with VHS tapes. The digital revolution saw an epic struggle between DVD and laser disk. DVD won. Towers of disks replaced those massive racks of VHS tapes. Not many years later, the new battlefield was between HD DVD and BlueRay. BlueRay beat its competitor. The internet is the new battlefield. In each of these cases, there was a consistent player that decided the technological direction the industry would go. There is a sinister reality as to why 8mm, VHS, DVD, BlueRay, and others beat their competitors. It was the porn industry that did it.

The first pornographic film appeared in the late 1800s. Since then, it has driven the media world to invent and innovate. It was the porn industry that backed 8mm and thus that technology reigned supreme for a while. When the porn industry almost wholesale backed VHS instead of Betamax, the writing was on the wall. The same happened with DVD and BlueRay. It was even the porn industry that pioneered the technology that allows for automated closed caption and invented online payment.

It is wrong to think of the porn industry as a passive option. Porn has a dark evangelistic side. It is aggressive and active everywhere men, and now increasingly women, are. Porn is not merely "out there." Porn is coming. It wants you and me and everyone you know. Even if you don't look at porn, you are using the technology that the porn industry backed.

If you've had the idea that through my years of ministry and Bible college, my porn consumption magically disappeared, that would be wrong. In those years, I was as involved with pornography as I ever was. Now, as the internet technology was maturing, so too was the content within. More privacy and anonymity meant the same thing for me as the rest of the young men my age — more hours on seedy sites watching and waiting for women to undress and do indecent acts.

There were times where I "struggled" with porn, but

most of the time, I just swam in it. I spent at least a few hours a week, seeking out internet material that would allow me to find a sexual outlet. That was happening whether or not I had a girlfriend. It happened on nights after I'd preached at church. It even happened after I had led Bible studies in which I encouraged youth to be pure. I recognized the sickening hypocrisy of it all.

There were times when I fought back. I ripped the ethernet cable out of the back of my computer one night. I realized that wouldn't be enough, so I tore the socket out of the wall. I had enough of the temptation and I wanted out, but porn is insidious. It always seems to find a way back in. It wasn't long before I was back at it.

Sometimes I would groggily come to my senses after being asleep for a few hours, only to realize that I was on the internet looking for naked girls. I always refused to use the word "addicted" in those years because that made it seem like something beyond my control. Early on, I wanted to stop, but as time progressed, I became more complacent with the rotten state of affairs.

Despite a few short seasons when I swore off pornography, I endured my roaring twenties never going for more than a month, maybe two, without looking at porn. The eventual numbness I experienced on the subject took me to some unusual conclusions.

I had taken some pretty straight forward verses

about lust and twisted them to mean what I wanted. For instance, Jesus said, "If you look at a woman with lust, you've committed adultery with her in your heart." That clearly means that lust and anything that results from lust is sin. However, I tried to pull a fast one on Jesus. I defined lust as "planning to have sex with a woman." I therefore reasoned that when I was looking at porn on video, I was not looking at women with whom I *could* ever be intimate. My twisted logic was that it didn't qualify as lust since I was never in the same room as these porn actresses, nor would we ever meet.

In addition to this, I calculated that it was possible to look at porn that was animated. I knew of guys who did. In this situation, there was no real person to lust after, so I extended this logic to live-action porn. I surmised that the actresses in porn clips were a kind of parody of real life. Therefore, I thought it shouldn't qualify as lust.

I always had my ticklish ears open for ideas that could alleviate my guilt. I wanted to feel free of the heavyweight that being a minister who looked at porn produced. In those years, I came across multiple arguments that sexual self-gratification was not a sin. The argument was, "The Bible doesn't specifically forbid the act."

Putting all of this together, I cautiously concluded that porn and its outcome was probably ok with God. It was a thin defense against the guilt I felt, though I was prepared to continue to build my blooming case. These were meager justifications that only partially staunched the growing wound that porn was creating in my life.

I was looking for an escape from the gnawing questions that the situation presented. I had often heard real Christians could not willingly live in sin. I wasn't sure exactly what constituted a willing life of sin, but by most definitions, I was living it. That didn't fit with my experience, though. I felt pretty sure that I was saved, especially because I was actively doing ministry, reading my Bible, and praying regularly. So if I could convince myself that porn was not a sin, then I could effectively get around the obvious logical dilemma.

One night I was lying in bed tired of the constant battle. I wanted to be free from the ever-present back and forth in my mind. My justification was beginning to tone down my guilt, but it wasn't a full-scale defense. I wanted to settle it once and for all, and resign myself to the outcome. If I could finalize my conclusion that porn wasn't a sin, I would continue guilt-free and stop worrying about it. It was an attractive option. I was excited because I thought I had found a reasonable solution that could free me from my moral torment. All that was left was to get divine approval for the plan.

I hit my knees and began to pray. I'm just going to admit that this was a weird prayer. It probably was not the weirdest prayer I've ever prayed, but it would make the top ten. I whispered these words to God, feeling like

I might be almost at an end to a long road of guilt.

"Lord, I feel like I see the truth. I can see now that this isn't a sin. But if I'm wrong—If it is a sin—please show me." With that, I reached for my Bible and let it fall open to a seemingly random verse. I rarely, if ever, had played this form of Bible roulette, but it seemed to be simply a formality at this point. I had already come to my conclusion. I could feel the weight lifting. I already knew what I would be doing that night. It was exciting to imagine a life lived the way I wanted to, without the nuisance of guilt and shame. The freedom was short-lived as my eyes fell to the verse on which my finger had landed.

"Do not be a slave to your own body..." it read. I seriously am not sure if this was God speaking to me, or if it was merely a fluke. Though the verse seemed to be too on the nose not to mean something, it struck at the deeper problem with my porn routine. Even if the act itself was not a sin, any bodily habit that enslaved me was wrong. I had to admit that I was not in compliance with that verse. I was a slave to my sexual appetite. I closed the Bible more than a little frustrated with God and embarrassed at my attempt to normalize a deplorable habit.

My house of cards fell apart, and my man-made justifications blew away with that simple phrase. I felt the raw pain of it all. I was addicted to porn. I was living with sin. It was a sin that I willfully allowed into my life regularly. I was such a hypocrite. I was such a fake. So many preachers had said that being a new creation in Christ meant that I should not be able to live like this. The reality hit like a brick to my jaw. If they were right, then I might not be saved. It never even occurred to me that they could be wrong.

LATVIA

I got a call from Clay, the missions pastor of a large church in Athens, Texas, one afternoon as another summer was approaching. I had never met him before, but he had gotten my name from a local youth minister that had me speak at his youth events.

"Hey, I'm organizing a mission trip to Latvia, and was wondering if you'd come and be our evangelist," Clay said after we got introductions and pleasantries out of the way.

"What's Latvia?" I said. Already my blood pressure was rising. I had a personal policy of saying yes to any speaking gig, but this was making me nervous. I had never left the continent before. International travel was an audacious prospect for me, but I didn't want to admit I was afraid.

"It's one of the small Baltic states in Eastern Europe. It was part of the former Soviet Union," he explained. That didn't make me feel any better. I had heard some pretty nasty stories about being thrown into the Gulag.

"Can we— Err, I mean— Is it legal to preach there?" I said this, knowing that I was showing my ignorance. I just wanted to be clear on what I was getting into. Clay took a long pause before he spoke, probably reeling from my lack of geographical knowledge.

"Yeah, of course. It's not only legal, but they are very open to the gospel. We've been seven times," he said. At that, my tension began to release. I already knew I would say yes, but I had just wanted to see if I should kiss my momma goodbye forever before going. He assured me that we'd come back alive, and I agreed. Before we hung up the phone, I was committed to being the trip evangelist for a mission to Latvia, and the best part was that the church would pay for my trip. He gave me one final bit of advice.

"Whatever you do, don't fall in love while we're there. The Latvian girls are beautiful. All of the women look like fashion models. We've had more than one young man fall hard for a Latvian lady," he said. I liked the sound of this trip already.

Latvia was a land of magic and beauty. The capital of Rega was a bustling city, but as we drove to Cesis, which would be our destination for two weeks, I watched the sprawling cityscape give up its rigid lines to domesticated farming land and then finally forested hills. The scenery was utterly green. Though snow blanketed the area a goodly portion of the year, it was also part of the fertile swath of countryside that had fed the Russian federation of states for decades. I could see why. Everywhere I looked was a blooming haven of vegetation.

Cesis was a proper town with a few pubs, restaurants, and a little under-attended church. The town's architecture was strongly reminiscent of medieval stone. Many of the buildings had stood their ground for centuries. A feudal era castle was one of the main features of the beautiful little corner of Eastern Europe. For a few bucks, tourists could climb the turret tower and look over the red clay roofs of the city. Spreading out below the castle was a mild meandering river that snaked through the gentle woods. I had imagined my first international mission trip would be in some dusty corner of Africa filled with squalor and poverty. It wasn't meant to be. This was like arriving in paradise.

Though the scenery was amazing, the people were more of a pleasant enigma than I had dreamed. Our team would spread out a blanket in the wooded patch near the gardened stream, and teenagers would suddenly materialize. There was rarely a time when we didn't have at least a dozen high school-aged kids following us around. They were eager to hear what we had to say and my translator assured me it was genuine interest.

I had thought we would have formal revival-style meetings where there was a designated preaching time.

Though we did that some, the most satisfying times were the impromptu meetings. One evening we were having dinner at a pub and pizza place near the city center. We had paid for pizza for two dozen teens. The place was busy with other patrons with whom we had no association. We sat at a long table with the twenty or so kids drinking the Latvian version of Coca Cola. At one point in the meal, and I'm not sure how he determined this, my translator turned to me and said, "It's time."

I knew what that meant. I was to stand and share the gospel. Right there in the middle of the pizza parlor, my translator and I stood, and we began to tell a full house of pizza-eating Latvians about Jesus. It was a rush of nerves and satisfaction. My heart beat like racehorse hooves as I did my best to explain what I knew about Jesus.

A day into the trip, I noticed that something was peculiar about the schedule. I didn't wear a watch, nor did I have a cell phone at the time. There was a bell tower in town which rang out the hour, but I hadn't paid much attention to it. As we returned to the little hostel outside of town, I asked one of the team members, "What time is it?" It felt like a very long day. She looked at her watch and reported.

"12:20 am," she said. My jaw could have hit the floor. The sun was still up, and the dusky light promised to swirl about the horizon for at least another hour.

"Sheesh, what time does it get dark around here?" I asked, trying to understand why the sun was so slow in its descent.

"It's dark from about 1:00 am to 4:00 am," she explained with a smile. "That's why we come this time of year. There's lots of daytime. That offered the maximum number of hours for us to evangelize. The other half of the year, the opposite was true. The long winter boasted days with only four hours of sunlight, while the nights lasted nearly twenty. It was no wonder that these Latvian kids wanted to get the most out of the summer sun considering the long months they were overspread in darkness.

One of our main projects in Cesis was to host a sports camp. For whatever reason, American basketball had become a Latvian fascination. We rented a sports center in town and taught them to play. We brought along a handful of basketball coaches from the United States. The kids would rotate through eight stations where they would learn the fundamentals of the game. One of the stations was mine, though what I was teaching them was something different altogether.

I had been in a basketball class in college, and I was by far the worst player. I wasn't there to teach them to dribble or run plays, (If basketball has plays— I'm not even sure). They would rotate to my station, sweating from their work out. They'd get a fifteen minute "water break" as I talked to them about Jesus.

Though it was a fantastic feeling to be talking to kids on the other side of the world about Christ, I was nervous at the same time. I was clear on the fact that Jesus died for sins and rose again. I didn't know what to tell the kids they had to do to receive the gift of salvation. Was it belief? Was it behavior? Was it repentance? I hid my lack of clarity behind a host of interesting illustrations and pseudo-spiritual stories.

The final weekend we were there, we held a "youth retreat." There was a recreational center outside the city, which was a former summer camp run by the Communists. It had long since been owned by a private party and was now a rentable venue for events. We chartered a large bus to carry about fifty Latvian teens to this retreat center. Over the weekend, we did an intensive youth function. We played games, sang songs, and talked to them about what Jesus had planned for their lives.

The final evening we were with them, I pulled out my most emotionally manipulative story. I talked to the kids about falling for a girl during college. She unexpectedly died that year. As the tears fell from their faces, I used the emotion of the moment to ask them to commit to Jesus. It was a cheap trick, but I had seen countless other speakers do it.

I had them bow their heads and close their eyes. Once again, I felt uncomfortable with what I was about to do, though I knew the team expected it. I knew Clay, who had invited me to come and paid for my trip, expected me to give an invitation. That was the moment they had been waiting for all week and I delivered.

I had them pray a sinner's prayer. I had them commit their lives. I had them raise their hands if they had prayed the prayer. I had them stand up and walk down front. In all twenty-one of those teens raised their hands, came down the aisle, and committed their lives to Christ. The experience left me with intense mixed emotions. I could see a kind of victory in it, though at the same time, I could see an impending defeat.

I had been taught that a person had to stick with the faith until the end of their life to be saved. I had been taught that even if a person professed faith in Christ, they could prove that they were never really saved if they didn't live a life of continuous Christian growth.

I knew that we would soon be leaving town. I knew that these twenty-one kids would soon be left behind, watching the Americans drive away. Without anyone to disciple them, it seemed like a hopeless prospect. The Americans would return in a year after the snow abated, and the days grew long, but would that be enough? Would they all abandon the faith by then?

The Apostle Paul once said that he planted, meaning he evangelized a group of people, and another person named Apollos watered, meaning he helped the new believers grow. Where was my Apollos? Who would disciple these young, eager believers in the days, weeks, and years after we left?

NON THE BAPTIST

When we got back into Cesis with the bus full of teens, there was an electric buzz in the air. On the way back, we talked to the kids about being baptized. It was the next logical step. They loved the idea and so we excitedly made plans to baptize the twenty-one who had spoken up about their new faith in Christ. We would do it at the local church, with whom we had a loose affiliation.

The small church in town that we had partnered with was one that we hardly had entered since we'd arrived. We had spent the week doing whatever we saw fit and thought the church had given us their blessing. The building itself was a miniature cathedral filled with the strange trappings of liturgical rites. The congregation consisted of about ten ancient frowns with people attached to them.

Our tires hit the cobbled main street of Cesis early Sunday morning. We took the teens who had converted to that little church. We announced with triumph that nearly two dozen kids had become believers in Christ, and now they wanted to be baptized. There was a flicker of hope in me. I was beginning to see a path for discipleship. This church could be the answer. They could be the Apollos, the stationary minster who continued the mission work that Paul had begun. They could water the seeds that we planted. At the moment of highest triumph, they tore our hopes apart.

"They said they won't do it," my translator explained. We were huddled up near the back pew, waiting to hear. Our faces fell as it sunk in what was happening.

"They won't do what?" Clay asked.

"They won't baptize the kids until they have come to church for at least a year." There was an audible groan and murmur from the entire American team. We had worked hard that week. We wanted to give these young believers the best chance of success in their newborn Christian life.

"But they have to! We—" one began.

"I'm telling you," our translator interrupted. "It's not going to happen. They're very stubborn." As he explained, the gnarly dented tubes of the out-of-tune pipe organ began to play. The service was starting. I was slated to preach, and I was in a boiling mood. I could not believe these stubborn people would refuse to water the seeds we had come so far and worked so hard to plant. I had planned to preach about something else, but I started to thumb through the pages of Acts, knowing I had a new subject for the morning's sermon.

When it came time for me to get up and speak, I opened to the story of the Ethiopian. It appears among the amazing stories in the book of Acts. The Apostle Philip shares the gospel with this Ethiopian guy, and as soon as the guy believes it, Philip baptizes him in the nearest body of water. He doesn't have to show a year's worth of commitment. He doesn't have to jump through any hoops. He gets baptized on the spot simply because he's convinced it's true.

Man, I let em' have it. It probably was the fieriest sermon I've ever delivered. I opened up my internal furnace and let the glowing embers pour out. I'm not sure if my translator toned down my blazing rhetoric, but I let them know in no uncertain terms that I disagreed with their decision and that they needed to baptize these kids.

The congregation that morning was a strange mixture. On one side, there were the beaming faces of these newly believing teens who had a growing fascination with Jesus. Their warm countenance could light any dark cathedral. On the other side of the room were the icy frowns of the stone-faced congregants. There seemed to be no compassion. They had watched their church struggle to fill even one pew for so many years that they had lost all hope in the next generation.

Our time was running out. After some consideration, we got the American team together and began to hatch a plan. Frustrated and annoyed by the old guard who stood sentry at the church, we began to imagine another way to get these new believers baptized. All we needed was some water deep enough to stand in.

There was a little pottery shop near the center of town where we met for one of our last Bible study times. We gathered with the new converts we had made, plus a handful of others. We announced to them that our last day in Latvia, we planned to baptize anyone who had put their faith in Jesus for salvation. It was exciting to see the smirk spread across multiple faces as the translator explained not only what we said, but what baptism meant.

The final day was one of joy and sorrow. The water was cold and I don't mean Texas-in-October cold. Despite the chattering teeth, we baptized the teens without a single one of the old church ladies in attendance. Their bright faces and warm responses let us know that our work was appreciated, if not by those at the church, at least by them. Wet hugs and exuberant expressions of faith needed no translator to be understood.

Our jet would be leaving in the morning, which

made the city-wide festival that took place our last night there, an extraordinary experience. Familiar sounds filled the air as a Latvian 'country' band played in the town square. I had thought that country music was a phenomenon unique to the American south, but apparently, it had caught on in this corner of Eastern Europe. As the band played deep into the night, and the dusky light clung to the edges of the sky far past two in the morning, we mingled in a tightly woven crowd of Latvians. We could almost pretend that this was our goodbye party, but in reality it was a festival that took place on that date every year. Most of the people in the square had no idea who we were and might never hear the gospel.

"Vai jūs vēlētos dejot?" Came the words from behind me. She had to shout to be heard over the thumping music. I didn't know Latvian, but I could understand the body language well enough. She was asking me to dance. I knew only her name and that she had spent the week listening and taking part in our Bible meetings. Laima was a beautiful girl with flowing black hair and the slender build of a fashion model. She reached out and wrapped her arms around me before I could respond. We moved with the music as she pulled me in close.

Clay was right; the Latvian women were gorgeous. He had told me not to fall in love. Laima was only a few years younger than me. I enjoyed the dance, but what I was feeling was far from love. I felt regret. As the music billowed through the square, I looked down at her face, not able to speak to her. If we could talk, maybe I would tell her what a disservice I had done to her and her people. We had shared the gospel and her friends had responded, though, in the morning, we would leave them to fend for themselves.

We spun around, holding each other close as if no one else was there. That's where my memory of the night ends as if Laima and Latvia itself evaporated into the mist of time. I wonder what happened to Laima. Did she marry, or have kids, or something else equally natural?

Leaving felt wrong, not because of Laima, or the others who had believed. Leaving felt wrong because of what I believed. If I really wanted to ensure that these people stayed in the faith, wouldn't I stay in Latvia? Why should I have the choice to return to the Bible Belt? Why should I have been born to a family that prays and goes to church and loves Jesus? I could hardly stand that we would leave them behind with nothing to ensure that they continued to follow Jesus. All I knew is what I had been told by other speakers, teachers, and preachers. If they didn't endure in the faith until the end of their lives, they would still end up in Hell. I also believed that God would now judge them more harshly if they fell away because they had now heard the gospel. I knew of no other alternative.

I went home feeling that what I had done was taken a European vacation paid for by Clay's church, in which I left my Latvian listeners worse off than I'd found them.

That placed a dark cloud over all of the mission trips I took part in for years to come. I saw no distinction between salvation and discipleship. Consequently, I couldn't see how any short term evangelistic effort was of any value. I would go on to do multiple international mission trips, all the while feeling this heavy burden of defeat.

THE PASSION

"If you can't feel the presence of God in this place, you should check your spiritual pulse!" I heard a sweating revival preacher say once. It frightened me. I was not all that moved by his preaching antics, which seemed surprisingly similar to a red-faced temper tantrum. I had known since I was a child that I didn't have the same emotional depth that others did, or at least I was not comfortable expressing it openly. I had things that moved me, but they rarely were what I found on the pages of a Bible, or what I heard sitting in the pew at church.

Around the years of my entrance into Junior college, a movie of massive proportions was approaching its release date. This movie was new hope in the dark land of emotional isolation where I lived. It promised to change me from the inside out. This film was a multi-million dollar undertaking in which focus groups and pre-release audiences alike wept profusely. Everyone who saw it spoke effusively of the deep emotional experience it represented. It was going to bring new spiritual enlightenment to my seared sentiment.

A master storyteller had envisioned the project and he was bringing it to life with all the power Hollywood had to offer. The movie was Mel Gibson's *The Passion Of The Christ*. I had placed so much hope on this movie, believing that I needed something to wake me from my emotional malaise. I strongly desired to connect the frayed wires of my sentimental center, to the rigid circuit board of my Spirituality. I was committed to the Lord, but I never wept about it, I never felt broken over my sin, and I didn't ever feel *the presence of the Lord* when the preachers said I should. Of course, a movie could change all that.

I anticipated this movie for months, hoping that finally, I would be able to break my emotional isolation and have some kind of *real* spiritual experience. The church I was going to at the time rented out an entire theater so that we could all experience the emotional massacre together. The girl I had a crush on rode with me to the screening. We had to sit on the front row, but at least we were together. I quickly realized this was not a hold-hands kind of movie. That's not to say that she would let me hold her hand in any case. It was an unrequited affection.

As the lights dimmed, I readied myself, determined to be focused on the experience. I pushed all unrelated thoughts out of my mind and opened myself up to whatever God might do in my heart.

As the brutality of Christ's trial and execution swelled to a fever pitch, the dark theater began to fill with sniffles. Right on cue. Mel had done his work well. The sobs were soft and singular at first. As the graphic depiction erupted into blood and violence, the cries grew into a symphony of weeping. There was an energy in the room. There was power. There was emotion.

Like Superman basking in the radioactivity of the yellow sun, I intended to soak up the crying and gain emotional superpowers. I expected to feel something deep and intense. It was supposed to gush like a river of passion or erupt like a volcano of sentiment. I sat and waited for my tear glands to begin pumping that salty fluid. That would prove I was *really* saved, that I *really* cared about my Lord, that I *really was* sensitive to the Spirit.

Unfortunately, I couldn't feel anything. I could see that others were having a mystical encounter with the divine. Still, I was left behind by a room full of emotional prodigies. The weeping increased and then died off as the resurrection approached. I was utterly disappointed. The audience even gave a standing ovation at the resurrection. I stood and clapped with them, but my heart was not in it. They had been taken on a metaphysical journey and delivered at the foot of the sacred. They had made an intangible pilgrimage and tasted the holy waters that flow from the throne of

God, while I stayed home and drank off-brand cola. I deflated entirely.

After the movie, those who had attended were scheduled to meet back at the church. Driving there, I hoped that my waterworks were yet to come. The entire congregation returned to the sanctuary for a time to process and pray about what we'd seen. The tears continued to flow for most. Soft music and low, warm lighting wafted incorporeal about the room. For the price of a movie ticket, these hundreds of people had touched the hem of the divine. For my ticket price, I regressed into an aloof emotional hermit. How is it that all of these people are having this powerful shared catharsis, and I'm feeling nothing, nothing at all?

I tried hard, but I couldn't muster the emotion that anyone else was experiencing. The only thing I felt was mad. I wanted what everyone had. They were all like a team who had worked hard for a victory and they were accomplishing it together.

I stood from the pew I occupied and marched down to the front of the sanctuary. I grabbed the pastor by the arm. He was a powerfully towering personality— Brother Andrews would have answers. He would know what was missing. He would see into my soul.

"I think there is something wrong with me," I said.

"What do you mean, Son?" He replied with a southern charm that usually would warm my countenance. I could see the characteristic redness and the tears that twinkled at the corner of his eyes.

"Everyone is moved to tears. I'm not. I think there's something wrong with me," I explained.

"Let's pray together, Son," he said as he placed his large hand on my bony shoulder. We knelt on the first step of the stage and prayed. For him, more tears flowed. For me, more nothing.

The entire experience was a disappointment. I had hoped on the promise of emotion, and it did not deliver. I came away believing that I was emotionally and spiritually incompetent. I believed that because believing the alternative was much too frightening.

BEFORE THE LORD

In the corner of the Bible Belt, where I grew up, there was this pervasive idea that faith equals fervor. Disregarding the fact that the two words have entirely separate etymologies and semantic domains, the cohabitation of these two terms never seemed all that questionable to my developing mind. In practice, it merely meant that you had not had a spiritual experience unless you had an emotional one. On fire, brokenness, godly sorrow, and total dependence on God was the vocabulary that bolstered the otherwise dubious conflation of emotion and belief.

At every youth and college event, the repeated refrain seemed to be: "Try harder— pray longer— go deeper— depend on God more." As any college student understands, life was changing and I had many decisions that stood before me. Being thrown unwillingly into the world of full-time adults was daunting. I wanted to be spoon-fed a step-by-step plan for my every move. The college ministers and event speakers waxed long on what they called "total dependence on God." That was how one's life was to be lived, looking to God for every step. Whether they meant this quite literally or not was rarely if ever enumerated. Pressuring college kids to depend on God would probably be much more effective if it accompanied some explanation of a method that would achieve this saintly lifestyle. Unfortunately, very few practical steps were offered. That left me to improvise.

"You need to stand naked before God if you want Him to hear your prayers." the man said from the stage. The occasion was another in a long line of pseudo-evangelistic revival-style events. The speaker was a guy from a few towns over. He was a real emotion vendor. I could feel the coming crescendo as if I'd heard the tune a thousand times. I listened intently, watching every move, seeing if I could use any of his tricks in my ministry. He repeated himself for effect. That was good; I could use that.

"Did you hear what I said? You have to stand before God naked if you want Him to listen to your prayers!" He was shouting now. On his second approach, the words had a sharper tone. No doubt, he meant *naked* as a metaphor for openness and transparency, but the idea intrigued me.

Why not? I thought. I often felt as if my prayers were bouncing off the ceiling anyway. I had long since reasoned that I lacked the fervor needed to be heard by God. Maybe this was it. Perhaps this would be my big breakthrough.

Finding a place to pray naked can be difficult. My older brother had moved out to go to a college out of town, but my parent's house still had three other people living within. Nudity was not acceptable in the house, even nudity of a spiritual nature. To complicate things, my bedroom didn't have a lock on the door.

I knew that I'd have to be careful as I began to remove my clothes for my first nude prayer session. I stripped down to my birthday suit and knelt right in front of the closed door of my room. That ensured that if someone tried to come in while I was having a naked convo with The Almighty, my body would block the door from opening. I kept my clothes close at hand in case I needed to come back to the land of the linen in a hurry.

At that time, dating was a subject up in the air. I wanted to have a serious relationship and I had my eye on a particular girl. Though I would have used other words than these, what I wanted was God to give her to me. That was the subject of my first bare-skinned plea to the Lord.

I reasoned that disrobing was a way to show God how serious I was about getting a positive response to my request. In my stark state, I begged God to lead me, which was code for "Force that girl I like to fall in love with me."

The seriousness with which I undertook this unclad invocation was unprecedented. It brought a new kind of zeal to my prayer life. It became almost unimportant what words I was saying as long as I was saying them au naturel. I did a few more sessions in my bedroom before it became clear that something was missing other than my clothes.

After many attempts, I was left pondering my birthday suit supplications. It would be flatly wrong to say the only thing I prayed for was a girlfriend. It did dominate much of my prayer time, but so too did many other life decisions. After a year of practice, I felt no closer to gaining what I had asked for than when I started. I began to consider how I might add fuel to the fire since the practice was growing mundane. In thinking over my naked prayer times, I realized the problem was my length.

My prayers were entirely too short. Each time I prayed, I would spend only fifteen to twenty minutes, begging the Lord for what I wanted. I realized that my exposed beseeching was only the first step. I needed to do as the spiritual giants often did. I needed to pray all night. My bedroom would not be an adequate place for such a ceremony. I would be too tempted to fall asleep.

I had never been caught praying naked, which

mitigated the excitement of the endeavor. I was becoming complacent and bored by the bare bottom begging. I was not an exhibitionist, but remember, I was trying to manufacture emotion. What stronger emotion is there than the fear of being caught with no clothes on? Isn't that exactly what dreams are made of? Still trying to get the girl, and have my life planned for me by the all-seeing (and probably disgusted) Father, I had another desire to add. I had come to idolize Christian speakers like Giglio, Piper, Chan, and Chandler. I put a spiritual spin on it, but ultimately I wanted to be a Christian celebrity. With these three requests, I planned my next leafless litany for a less private locale.

After my family had gone to bed, I left my bedroom and made my way to the garage. My parents had allowed us to convert it into a recording studio a few years before. Among the microphones and guitars, I took off my clothes. This within itself was a risky move since the door to the garage had a glass window. My mom's sleeping pattern was erratic, and my brother was known for waking in the night, unable to sleep, he would go out and play his guitar for an hour.

Kneeling naked in the studio, I began to pray. With enthusiasm and passion, I begged the Lord for the things and people that I wanted. Pursuing selfish desires in a spiritual way somehow smooths the sharp edges until they become ostensibly appropriate. Though now I can hardly imagine anything more inappropriate.

I wanted the Lord to give me some kind of Christian sanctioned celebrity status, a mate, and a step-by-step life plan. Among the guitars, I was praying the most rock-n'-roll prayer possibly. I wanted sex, fame, and a management deal, and in true rock-n'-roll style, I did all this without any clothes on. To top it off, I fulfilled those famous words of rock-n'-roll legend, Lionel Richie. I went *"all night long."*

IN THE BUFF

For a semester, I attended a university in Dallas. Living on campus was incredibly lonely since most of the students I met during the week were commuters. My dorm was a closet-sized room with three stinky college students crammed inside. Our bathroom was shared by six. Consequently, I spent long hours alone on the edge of campus late into the night.

I had my favorite private spots at the college. Sometimes I would carry my guitar along and play or I'd write in my pocket journal. Often I took long walks while thinking and praying. That was not because I was uber spiritual, but instead, because I was utterly desperate for companionship.

I had left the girl I had a crush on back home. I had begged the Lord to force her to fall in love with me for over a year now. God didn't seem to be getting the picture and I was getting desperate. Living two hours away from my unrequited love meant that I was a sulky sack of sorrow most of the time. I wouldn't say I was depressed but focused. The Lord heard from me often on the subject.

My desire to be a Christian celebrity had not waned either. Every week, the Christian university did a big passion-style event. Most weeks, the famous duo Shane and Shane played the worship, and a well-known speaker named David Edwards preached. I had a late dinner with David one Thursday night after hours. His stories of living on the road and speaking to thousands only fueled my desire to become a Christian celebrity.

Other nights of the week, I paced the perimeter of the campus, preferring the private stretches of pasture that the college had not yet developed. My favorite place was a little strip of land next to Sky Lake. It was hardly a lake—a small pond at best. The residence of the university's president was on the other side of the lake and was the only building anywhere nearby. Before the campus developed in that direction, there were no lamp posts or night lights. I would spend long hours down by the pond. I assumed no one ever noticed my presence since it was usually by night I visited the little body of water.

Throughout that semester, I had been keeping a journal. Though 'journal' is not the right word for it. It was more of a devotional booklet confessing my pining for the girl I had left back home. It was like my own little apocryphal book of worship to a foreign female god though I didn't see it that way at the time.

After months on campus, I was feeling that old wound; I was a victim of God's indecisiveness. He had not given me fame, a girlfriend, or a plan. I rose from the top bunk and slipped outside. It was some time after midnight and I needed a walk. I marched toward my favorite old spot in my untied combat boots and plaid pajama pants. I was tired of waiting and I needed to show the Lord how serious I was about getting my prayers answered.

"Are you even listening to me?" I whispered against the breeze as I headed to my destination by the pond. The sky was moonless and the faint twinkle peeked through the glow of city lights. I was confident that everyone was in bed and had imagined that I was the only one awake on campus. I plopped down in the field west of the lake which needed to be mowed. Looking up at the sky, I begged God once again to give me what I wanted. I'm sure I used more eloquent words to hide my nefarious desires, but in retrospect, I was like the squeaky kid asking for a Ferrari when I didn't even have a driver's license.

I thought back to the previous year. I had spent hours praying naked in the safety of my parent's house. What little effect it had on my life. A spark of ingenuity brightened my mind. At first, I had only prayed naked in short bursts. Then when I realized that hadn't worked, I tried praying all night. Was it possible that I still hadn't mastered the craft of beseeching in the buff?

I glanced across the lake at the president's residence, certainly the distance would be enough to hide my shadowy presence. The late hour made it unlikely he was awake. Maybe he wasn't even home. To the north, about a quarter of a mile, there was a campus guard station that was supposed to have security personnel at all times. I wasn't concerned about it either; I had stolen to this patch of pasture by the dark of night. About thirty yards to the west was a road. I surmised that even if traffic were to pass, they would not be able to see what I was about to do in the unlit field.

Even at the thought of what I planned, my heart began to race. I glanced down at my untied combat boots. *Am I really going to do this,* I thought. "Yes," came a whisper that hardly seemed to be my own. I pushed one off with the toe of my other boot. It thumped on the ground like the sound of a ball and chain. It was like liquefied liberation pumping in my veins.

Glancing around me once more, I removed my shoes, then my shirt. I was committed now. With one final definitive removal, I found myself in a field completely naked. My breath was now rising to match the speed of my pounding heart. I spun over, knelt in the prickly grass, and began to pray.

One author has written that we need to be radical for the Lord. I don't know if this is what he meant, but this was the most radical thing I could bring myself to do. I prayed with fervor under heaven and the stars as divested of cover as anyone has ever been. I was searching for emotion, passion, intensity. I got all of that suspended naked in that glorious moment, though I also got something else. I got noticed. That was not surprising since the night was no longer moonless.

On the road, only twenty yards to the west, a car was driving slowly, too slowly. *Don't panic,* I thought. *They're just taking a midnight cruise.* I watched as the vehicle, a large SUV, slowed. As it passed under a streetlamp in the distance, I recognized the dreaded black and white design. It was a police cruiser, and it was coming my way. *Ok, maybe it's time to panic.* I grabbed my clothes, not sure what to do. If I ran, I'd have to do it like a super bowl streaker. If I took the time to put them back on, I might get caught.

I eyeballed the police car as it slowed and pulled into the shoulder. *Maybe he's just setting up a speed trap,* I thought. I tried to convince myself that his untimely stop had nothing to do with me. However, that theory was dashed to pieces when a massive spotlight clicked on.

"Lord, help me!" I said in a whisper. It was probably the most sincere prayer I've ever prayed. See praying naked does work! I don't know if the Lord helped me or not, but if He did, His help came in the form of speed and dexterity. I could not stand up as the spotlight was scanning overhead. The grass was just tall enough to conceal me if I remained in a prone position. I rolled over to my back in the prickly hay, thrust my naked pelvis in the air, and yanked my underwear up. I then took up a fetal position and reached for my shoes. They went on easy. The scratch of the grass reminded me that I would need to put my pants on, but they wouldn't fit over my boots. Reversing the order, I got my pants and shirt back on and returned to my shoes last in order.

With all the rustling in the grass, I'm surprised that the officer didn't find me. I stayed low until the threat was gone. To this day I don't know who called the cops, Maybe I was wrong about being undetected, and the president could see me from across the lake.

I can imagine the scene. The president gets out of bed to get a midnight snack. He glances out the kitchen window as he has a glass of milk. In the half-lit glow of the sky, he views a lewd moon in the distance across the lake. It's a college campus, so he knows what it means.

Ring, ring, ring. "Police department, how can I help you?"

"Hello, officer. It looks like a couple of college kids are having a roll in the hay down by the lake. Do you mind breaking it up?"

"Sure thing."

I was having a roll in the hay alright, but wouldn't the officer be quite befuddled to find that I was doing it all by myself?

When the threat of arrest finally passed, I snuck

back to my dorm room, thankful not to be in handcuffs. Sometime after that, there was a campus curfew and new shoes, shirts, and pants dress code announced. I'm sure there was no relationship to the anonymous naked prayer warrior.

Realizing that I nearly got arrested for indecent exposure offered me surprising clarity. I began to see that I had gone in a strange and illegal direction with my spirituality. After that night, I never prayed naked again.

The influences that had driven me to that spot in the pasture were challenging to untangle. I had spent years hearing teachers and preachers bellowing about zeal, passion, sacrifice, and living out a radical Christian life. What could be more radical than praying naked below the college president's back window? Though it was the ambiguity of those instructions that led me to this nudist notion in the middle of nowhere.

It was like following a stranger's directions down an unknown road for hours only to discover that it is a dead-end. After turning around and making the arduous trip back, it leaves one ever skeptical of any direction giving stranger.

I had been trying with all the strength in me to experience something, anything. I *had* felt something, but it was only the racing heart that any petty criminal experiences. It left me wondering if it was all fake. Was there any emotional experience that would satisfy? The letdown cast such a long shadow; I would come to doubt any emotional experience for years to come.

ONCE SAVED

Most of the friends I had were either in music or youth ministry. Some of them were in both. I had a buddy who had taken a ministry job at a church one town over. He was primarily a music minister, but he was good with students as well. He had never studied at seminary or even Bible college, but as I said, he was a great singer.

He invited me to preach at his church, Red Oak Fellowship, regularly. I had spoken there probably five times for both youth events and Sunday morning services. I knew many in the student ministry by name and was building a relationship with the congregation. When he called me one Friday afternoon, I could hear the concern in his voice.

"Man, I stuck my foot in my mouth," he said.

"What do you mean?"

"I was teaching last Wednesday," he explained with a note of trepidation. He paused as if he didn't want to tell me what happened.

"Yeah?" I prompted. "That's your job." I was trying to bring some humor, but he didn't take the bait. Clearly something had happened that unsettled him.

"I got into some hot water with the parents of some of my youth," he said.

"Really? What happened?"

"So, I was teaching, and I started talking about salvation. I got on the subject of *once saved always saved*." He took a breath, which indicated we were almost to the problematic part. "I said that it wasn't enough to pray a prayer that there had to be a life change. Some of the parents came and cornered me later and griped me out. I'm afraid I might get fired."

"Wow, that's brutal." I felt terrible for him. It was not entirely surprising. *Once saved always saved* is a controversial topic in many of the churches in the Bible Belt. There are multiple definitions of the term, which complicates the debate. It's not a simple task to craft a coherent thought on the subject. It's not the kind of issue anyone should try to answer without thinking through the logical implications. My friend had stepped into a bear trap without even knowing it.

I could relate to his situation because I had struggled with the same issue. So much of the confusion throughout my life came down to this one single word, *assurance*. Could a person who claims to have faith, but then lives like the Devil really be saved? Does Jesus assure salvation even to those who live a life of sin?

That was one of the great battles of my thought life and I wasn't exactly winning. I found myself often repeating famous Bible teachers like Grudem, Carson, and Sproul, but I was positive I had not gotten to the bottom of the issue. I could recite pithy pious lines, but something was missing in my understanding. Something didn't line up. That's why I avoided speaking on the subject publicly, and my buddy could have benefited from the same policy.

"Man, I'm sorry to hear that. I wouldn't want to be in your shoes," I said, trying to show some sympathy.

"Well, I was hoping you could help, actually," he said without missing a beat.

"Of course! What can I do?"

"You're the most knowledgable person I know on these kinds of subjects except my uncle, and he's out of town. I was wondering maybe you could come do a question and answer session with the students and parents next Wednesday night," he said.

I should have said, *are you crazy?* He had just fallen into this deep dark pit with spikes at the bottom, and now he was asking me to jump into it with him. I knew, even at that moment, that I wasn't really at a place to answer questions about *once saved always saved* with personal conviction. Of course, I could quote the famous reformed preachers on the subject, but was that really what they needed? The whole thing was as radioactive as Chernobyl and I should have proceeded with extreme caution. I should have asked him why the pastor of Red Oak Fellowship couldn't do the Q and A. It should have sent up red flags that he wanted a guest speaker in his early twenties from out of town to come and tackle these big questions.

"Of course, I'll come do a Q and A!" I said with gusto. I should have run for cover, but instead, I agreed to charge in with him. It was an invitation to a speaking gig, after all. With my voracious appetite for recognition, I had a personal policy not to turn down gigs.

What's more, it stroked my unhealthily bloated ego that he'd want me to come and help him sort out this difficult situation. I was so ambitious that I couldn't turn it down. I was so arrogant that I thought I could handle it without even preparing.

I was dense enough to look forward to the night. The stage, which I had spoken from multiple times before, was set up differently. There was a table and two chairs. The room was dark except for the stage lights. My buddy sat across the table from me and conducted an interview. It was like a churchy talk show but without the laughs, and with the added pressure that if it went poorly, he might get fired. He opened the evening with a promising introduction.

"Tonight is about getting your questions answered. Any question you have about Christianity that no one has been able to answer, write it down and pass it up, and Lucas will answer it," he said. Why not have them write down questions about astrophysics, quantum mechanics, and neuroplasticity while we're at it? Nothing starts a church service like overselling the guest speaker.

The students and parents began to write questions on index cards and pass them up to the front. Why they thought a kid in his early-twenties was going to have any answers, I still don't know. The questions began to find their way to the stage. The first few were predictable.

"How do you know God exists?" my co-host read aloud.

I answered with the fine-tuning of the universe, coupled with our inability to explain away Jesus. Whether it satisfied the questioner, I have no idea.

"Ok. Next question. How far is too far to go with my girlfriend?"

I could have groaned. I *would* rather answer the quantum mechanics questions than that one. I told the kids what I had heard from a speaker in college. "Imagine your girlfriend. Now in your imagination, draw a box with the bottom below her knees, the sides at her shoulders, and the top at her neck. Don't touch anything inside the box until you're married." The answer was not exactly from the Bible, but it got a laugh, so we moved on.

It went on like this for probably about an hour. I

now know that the most liberating phrase in the human language is, *I don't know.* I should have used that phrase often that night, but it didn't come out of my mouth once. I pretended to have a prepared answer for every question that came in. What I lacked in knowledge, I made up for with empty chatter and punch lines.

Somewhere toward the end of the night, we exhausted all the questions passed forward. I knew there was at least one more question. No one had written this one. It was the question that I had been brought there to answer. My buddy looked down at one of the cards as if it were just another write-in.

"What about once saved always saved? Can a person say they have faith but have no life change, and still be saved?" he asked. I stood from my chair and stepped to the edge of the stage. The wireless mic was heavy in my hand. I should have said, *I don't know. Thank you, and goodnight.* That would have been the most honest thing I could say at that moment. Instead, I leaned back on my years of preacher jargon.

"Great question. Salvation is by faith alone in Christ alone. It's a free gift. You can't do anything to earn it, and you can't lose it. However, if you willingly live in sin, that proves that you never were really saved in the first place. You see, salvation is a free gift, but it will cost you everything. If you truly have it, you can never lose it. If you lose it, you never truly had it. So, yes, I believe in once saved always saved, but I might say it this way.

Once you're *really* saved, you are always saved, but there are many people who think they're saved and really aren't."

Even as it was coming out of my mouth, I knew there was a logical problem with it. If salvation is free, it can't also be costly, but I'd heard so many preachers say it's both, so I was just repeating what I heard. I knew that based on what I had just told them that there was no way to have assurance until after you're dead, but I also knew that the Apostle John said that we can *know* that we have eternal life. I knew that telling people that salvation was a free gift but that they had to exhibit *life change* to prove they are *really* saved was contradictory. Life change is better behavior, following the rules, doing good works.

Jesus said, "Don't throw your pearls to the pigs because they'll turn and trample you." No problem, I was throwing mud to the sheep and to my amazement, they seemed to eat it up. That audience should have drug me outside and stoned me to death for the contradictory incoherencies I had just spewed. I had babbled on with empty platitudes and hidden my own confusion behind convoluted enigmas. They didn't stone me. They didn't even argue. They accepted what I had to say. They even seemed to enjoy the slew of obliquities.

It felt good to be appreciated, but there was a dark cloud over me for doing what I did. Even if they hadn't seen my inconsistency, I did. I knew I had dealt them a cheating hand of cards. I had dodged the real question with slick phrases that were emptied of all meaning as soon as they escaped my mouth. I wanted to share the truth about the Gospel, but it always seemed out of reach. After all, I was now the Bible answer guy apparently, and I knew my answers could be dismantled by clear reason. What a scary thought. I didn't realize it at the time, but this was the beginning of a long slide downward.

ILLUSTRATION

There were a handful of illustrations and analogies that I had picked up during my youth ministry days. I had used these clever-sounding parables at the climax of sermons and Bible lessons. They were part of my shiny tool kit of preacher sayings. They had aroused interest and intrigue from my audiences, but the gilding had begun to tarnish. After being in ministry for about seven years, I was no longer sure they were of value. One of these illustrious illustrations, which I'm sure you've heard, was the wheelbarrow illustration. It goes something like this.

"Let's say that I strung up a tight rope across Niagara Falls. I then took a wheelbarrow and carefully balanced it on the tight rope. With ease, I pushed that wheelbarrow across the tight rope without falling. After seeing that, would you believe that I could do it again? " Most will say, "yes."

"Now, let's say that I invite you to get in the wheelbarrow and go for a ride as I push you across that tight rope. Would you be willing to do that?"

At this point, most will fidget a bit because it sounds both frightening and unwise. The speaker then gives the application. "That's what it's like to trust Jesus. It's not enough to know he can save; you have to get in the wheelbarrow."

I admit that I had used this illustration to explain salvation a number of times when I was speaking on a regular basis. I liked it because it was vague enough to hide that I wasn't sure what was required for salvation. As I was approaching my mid-twenties, the analogy began to unravel on me. *What exactly does the wheelbarrow ride represent?* I was questioning everything, and no sacred cow was too holy to escape being dissected.

There was another analogy that I heard quite often in the years leading up to my twenties. It was the chair illustration. It went something like this.

"Faith is like sitting in a chair. It's not enough to believe that the chair will hold you. Faith is when you actually sit in the chair."

Once again, this illustration was probably valued for its power of obfuscation. Though it was supposedly designed to illuminate some biblical idea, it did nothing but hide the truth from plain sight. Was faith so mysterious that it could not be explained by normative definition? Why was the substance so elusive that it required enigmatic illustrations? I had begun to think that these types of obtuse metaphors made the meaning at least once removed from the audience's understanding. If I couldn't understand it, certainly there were others.

One Sunday, I was visiting a church in Tyler, TX. The youth minister was speaking. He was passionate and interesting to listen to. I could see why he had a booming student ministry. He even had long hair, an ambiguous fashion statement that could be simultaneously associated with Jesus' hairstyle, and a rebellious teen.

I don't remember the subject of his sermon, but I do recall that he used the chair analogy. "It's not faith until you actually sit in the chair," he said as if it made perfect sense. Maybe to some, it did, but to me, it stuck out like a twice-hammered, black-nailed sore thumb. His entire sermon had led up to that point. He finally was dispensing his sage wisdom and he used the chair illustration to do it.

In my younger years, I would have wandered out without question. I would have assumed the speaker knew something I didn't and I wouldn't want to embarrass myself by asking a dumb question. At this point, though, I had begun to suspect the impossible. I had started to think some preachers were saying things from the stage that they couldn't really define or explain. I was nursing the notion that these kinds of illustrations were not actually designed to illuminate the truth, but instead, hide the inconsistencies of the message.

I worked my way to the front at the end of the message. There was a line of congregants shaking the minister's hand and congratulating him on his *wonderful* message. After waiting in line, I shook his hand, thanked him for the message, and asked as simple a question as I could.

"In the chair illustration, what exactly does the *sitting down* represent? I mean, I want to make sure I've sat in the chair, so how do I do it?" I asked. I didn't portray any animosity in my demeanor. I certainly didn't mean any disrespect, but the question must have bothered him for the response he gave.

"Thanks for keeping me on my toes," he said before turning and abruptly walking straight away. I wondered if he was going to get a chair to demonstrate. Nope, I watched him strike up a conversation with someone else. He had turned his back on me without giving an answer. Had I offended the guy, had I said something inappropriate or was it possible that he didn't know either. As I look back on it now, I realize it's a tricky question. The wheelbarrow analogy shares the same trickiness.

Sitting in the chair and *riding in the wheelbarrow* apparently, represent faith. The illustrations are supposed to demonstrate that faith is something more than just mentally agreeing with certain facts. So, I wanted to know what the *'something more'* actually was. It seemed as if there should be a readily available answer.

In reality, the definition stands between a rock and a hard place. If you say that *sitting in the chair* is changing your lifestyle and doing good works, then you've just established a good-works-for-salvation market place. You'd effectively be buying your salvation by right living. If it's something more than mere mental activity but something less than good works, then it leaves the answer in a meaningless neutral zone where there exists nothing but the elusive vagaries of circular reasoning.

Some try to tackle this difficulty with the introduction of emotion and will. Supposedly this helps split the hairline division between sitting and not sitting in the chair. The apparent distinction is often explained as *head faith* and *heart faith*. In those years, I often heard preachers say, "Many people miss heaven by 18 inches, the distance from the head to the heart." I recently measured the distance from my head to my heart, and it wasn't anywhere near 18 inches. With an 18-inch head-to-heart distance, a person would have to be Goliath size. Though, that is the smallest of the difficulties with this *head* and *heart* illustration.

Though the youth minister was not able to answer the question, others have. They say that *sitting in the chair* or *riding in the wheelbarrow* represents when the belief moves from your *head* to your *heart*. Once again, this definition sounds meaningful, but when a clear difference between these two types of faiths is explained, they share the same confounded endpoint.

Emotions are a function of the mind. Passion does not literally take place in our aorta or left ventricle. Others have tried to explain that *heart faith, sitting in the chair,* and *riding in the wheelbarrow,* is when your beliefs work their way not only into your emotions but into your will. This always seemed to be simply a cleverly disguised way of saying, you'll do good stuff if you've *really* experienced faith.

In those years, I heard a preacher say that one way to determine if you're *really* saved is, "Check and see if you love Jesus more than sports, cars, your career, or your hobbies." This preacher, who has become quite famous now, would end his bit by saying, "What does your heart say about Jesus?" He placed the path of salvation through the heart, supposedly where the emotions and will power lived.

I always had a hard time with that. On what scale am I supposed to determine what I love more? In the end, I could only judge by my actions and works, but supposedly salvation isn't given on the basis of actions and works.

For years I was bathed in a constantly cascading waterfall of strange cliches, oblique illustrations, and obscure analogies. The result left me feeling like there were no answers that lay beneath these carefully constructed distractions. Faith and salvation's requirements couldn't be defined any more than a mist can be grasped in hand. I wanted to understand how all of these aspects fit together, but there were no clear and consistent answers as far as I could tell.

COLD
SEMINARY

I needed answers. I had lived with a theological limp for years. Bible college worsened the hobble. Being in ministry meant that I had to hide the hitch in my step. I had one last hope. I imagined, as naive as it may seem, seminary would be the hospital that could finally apply the healing bandage to my bewilderment. By now, I was crawling toward a fork in the road. It was like I had broken bones that had healed back together incorrectly. I would either get my confusion set right, or I would take another path in life.

My dad worked at the junior college I went to, and my mom was employed by the university from which I received my bachelor's degree. That meant that college was free of charge from my first class until they handed over my diploma. I didn't have any family members that worked at a seminary, so the only way to enroll was to either win the lottery or marry a rich widow. Neither seemed likely.

I didn't have the money, and I didn't want to take out a loan. Fortunately, I was working at one of the largest churches in Tyler, TX. I don't remember how it came about, but the administration of the church offered to pay for me to attend the seminary of my choice. I collected the $1000 from the church and enrolled in my first class at the seminary, which I considered the most prestigious. It was in Dallas, about two hours' drive from where I lived.

I enrolled in a single class, Evangelism. I had hung my hope on this new educational pursuit. This evangelism class would finally set things right for me. Unfortunately, there was only one time-slot that I could take Evangelism. I was on the roll for the 8:00 AM session. Since I lived two hours away, this meant I had to leave my house at 4:30 AM twice a week. This departure schedule would allow for Dallas morning traffic and a stop at MacDonald's. It didn't bother me. I was motivated. This class was going to be my rehabilitation.

The first class was on a cold day in January. I bundled up like the kid in *A Christmas Story*. I let my 1994 Jeep Cherokee warm for a few minutes before I hit the road. In the dark morning hours, the streets were abandoned. By the time I was nearing the outskirts of Dallas, I had noticed a strange environmental phenomenon. There was precipitation, but it wasn't wet. Little particles were flying through the air, but they didn't splash on the windshield as I expected.

I know it sounds like I'm exaggerating, but I didn't realize it was snow. Being a Texas boy, it just didn't compute. I thought it was strange that all of the other cars on Interstate-20 were creeping along far under the speed limit. I zoomed past, feeling the exhilaration of the first day of school.

Near the Forney exit, my wheels became unacquainted with the pavement. It happened so fast I didn't have time to react, except to shout out, "Lord, save me!" The Jeep was still moving at seventy miles per hour but was now turned entirely perpendicular to the road. It's a good thing that it was only 5:20 AM because I certainly would have hit another car on my trajectory had I been in traffic.

I slid across two lanes, the shoulder, the grassy median, and smashed into the center divider. The collision sent my car spinning in the opposite direction only to stall out 100 yards down the road. I was stuck in the middle of the ice-covered highway. I glanced sideways and saw headlights bearing down on me through the driver's side window. I reached for the keys and tried to crank the engine. It groaned like a dying donkey, not because it wouldn't start but because it was still running. That's what I love about a Jeep. It's built for war.

The lights were on top of me now. They had lost all stopping power on the frozen road. I pressed my foot to the floor, something I would never do unless my life depended on it. The moment qualified for maximum thrust. I had to get my Jeep off the road in a hurry, or I would be reduced to a bloodstain in the snow. The back tires whined as they ground into the smooth ice. An inch at a time, the Jeep fishtailed as I did my best to guide it toward the adjacent ditch. I narrowly escaped the road as an eighteen-wheeler zoomed by at fatal speed.

It had happened in a matter of seconds and my body had responded almost entirely without my conscious mind taking it in. I breathed for a moment now that I was semi-safe in the ditch. I jumped out of the car to survey the damage. Stepping back, I let out a shout of joy.

"Whoo, hoo!" Fist pump. "Thank you, Lord!" I ran my fingers across my open mouth. *Oh good, I still have all my teeth,* I thought. I was glad I hadn't sustained a life-altering injury, but my Jeep was in a sad state. The back window had popped out intact like the lid to a Tupperware in the microwave. The full sheet of glass was lying on the ground but was still connected by the rubber gasket that had previously held it in. The front right quarter panel had imploded on contact with the median, and the back hatch looked like wadded-up foil. I would find out moments later that the impact had somehow broken the heater. I thought this was a strange irony at the time.

I put the Jeep in four-wheel drive and rolled slowly toward the next exit. Too scared to get on the highway again, I kept my wheels on the grass as I puttered forward. When I finally got to the paved overpass, I reluctantly pulled onto the cold hard surface and headed up the exit ramp. It took me another few minutes to identify the grinding sound. The missing window dragged along the icy blacktop by the remaining rubber gasket. It would have been perfect for a snow day sled. The heaterless jeep was turning frigid, and I was now missing the back end of the car. That fifteen-minute ride was the coldest of my life.

Forney had one small hotel near the highway. My car limped into the parking lot like a scene from a Griswold movie. The snow was thickening and I determined that I'd have to spend some time in this little town. It wasn't until the clerk had reserved my room that I realized I didn't have my wallet. Had I forgotten it? Had I lost it in the crash? I was beginning to wonder if God didn't want me to go to seminary.

After all the effort to arrive on time to my first day of class, the seminary was closed for snow. I drove back home at 15 miles per hour. Weirdly, this was not the first time I'd made a multi-hour trip at such a slow speed. I was in a ponderous mood. Did it mean something? Was it God? Was it Satan? Or was it just weather?

My Jeep was no longer roadworthy. Once home, a mechanic friend convinced me to buy another broken down Jeep and use it for spare parts for the repair. For four hundred bucks, I found a blue Jeep that was only a few years older than my red one. It would ultimately take me months to get my vehicle back in good enough shape to use on the road. It would wind up being a very patriotic blend of red and blue body parts.

Word went out among my parent's friends that I had a wreck and was sans transportation. Mrs. Bellous, a sweet octogenarian who still gave piano lessons to kids in Kilgore, had a 1987 Buick Lesabre that she no longer could drive on account of her failing eyesight. Through the grapevine, she notified me that I could use the car as long as I needed it. She was thrilled to help out a seminary student.

It was originally gold but had greyed from the years of oxidation. It did not like going anywhere near the speed limit, which was fine by me considering my near scrape with death in my previous vehicle. By the next class day, I was back on the road. My 4:30 AM drive went off without a hitch.

EVANGELISM

I slid into my unassigned seat for my 8:00 AM evangelism class. I like to think I was more excited about this class than anyone else there. I assume that many of the students had to take it as part of their core curriculum. For me, this was my one class, and I had handpicked it from among many tantalizing options.

Making up for lost time, the professor gave his first assignment on the first day. We were to make an attempt at evangelism in the real world and write a paper about it. I was excited to get started, but it seemed to me that there was something missing. We were in this evangelism class to learn how to evangelize. If we already knew how, why would we be taking the class. Certainly, the professor, in his great and unmatched wisdom, knew what he was doing.

After going over the syllabus and looking around campus, I drove home feeling as if I hadn't learned anything yet. On the two hour drive home, I pondered what I would do for my project. I didn't want to repeat what everyone else was going to do, which was probably sit with a friend and talk to them about the Bible. I wanted to do something that would attract attention.

By the time I got home, I had a plan. I stopped by Hobby Lobby and bought a large piece of poster board. I printed out letters and taped together a poster that read, *Jesus came to save the world, not condemn it.* I took the poster to the busiest corner in my home town and held it up over my head for about an hour as cars passed. Some people honked, others waved, but other than that, I don't know that it had any effect. The next week I headed back to class with my report in hand. I was confident that I had taken the most radical approach, even if my effectiveness was questionable.

Coming from a family of graphic designers, I had chosen to lay my paper out in the format of a magazine. It had pictures of the intersection where I stood and of the sign itself. When I handed it to the professor, he noticed that it didn't fit the seminary's style for papers. On receiving it, he said, "Doing something different is risky because it brings attention to your project. It better be extra good." I smiled and sat down, not sure if it qualified as extra good, but it certainly qualified as different.

After a few weeks of class, something surprising occurred to me. The subject of the class lectures and the reading material was about delivery and presentation.

We discussed the way in which a revival ought to be conducted, how cross-cultural evangelism had often gone wrong, and relational approaches to sharing the Gospel. Through all of this, however, we had not talked about what the Gospel actually included.

I had questions that I wanted to be answered. Does a person have to behave to stay saved? Is sin a sign a person isn't saved? Can someone know for sure they have been saved? Most importantly, what does someone have to do to be saved? We had talked endlessly on different approaches to present the Gospel, but we hadn't yet discussed what the Gospel actually is. It didn't help me to know what intonation to use in a tent revival if I didn't know what words I was supposed to intone.

"Are there any questions?" The professor asked. "Yes?" he said, pointing to me. I'm not sure what he had been talking about, and I'm certain my question didn't have anything to do with it. The whole class looked in my direction.

"What exactly is the Gospel?" I said. I was almost sure that my question didn't really capture what I was trying to discover. "I mean, when we share the Gospel, what are we supposed to say."

It only occurred to me after the fact that the room was filled with people who probably found this question too basic for a seminary-level education. In my younger years, I would have worried about such trivialities. No longer! I was a drowning man looking for something to keep me afloat. In my increasingly desperate state, I didn't care what people thought of my infantile question. The class had cost me a lot. In addition to my wrecked jeep, I had been getting up at 4:30 AM and driving eight hours a week to find the answer. I wanted to know what I was missing.

"Ok," he said as if this fundamental question was an inappropriate interruption. In fact, it probably was. Who knows what he had actually been lecturing on. He held his right hand in the air and began to tick off a step by step plan for gaining eternal salvation. I ducked my head and began to write everything that came out of his mouth.

"First, they have to understand that salvation is a free gift received by faith, apart from good works. They must admit that they are a sinner, believe Jesus died for them, repent of their sins, commit to living their life for Christ, turn their life over to the Lord, and confess their faith to someone." He stared at me with an *"any more questions,"* look.

"Ok, thanks," I said, though I didn't feel grateful, This was the same type of inconsistent presentation that had long ago left me dissatisfied. The professor continued the lecture that I had interrupted. I began the slow descent into my own cave of brooding. I felt betrayed by the professor. No, that wasn't quite it, the seminary had let me down. That still didn't quite capture it. Christendom had used me for her purposes, all the while promising clear answers that never came. Christianity had claimed to be the most reasonable source of answers in this life and the life to come. My experience was that the most prestigious seminary I could ever hope to study at was as confused as any small town tent revival preacher.

I began to scribble on the page next to where I had jotted the professor's gospel presentation. If salvation is a free gift, then why did it require commitment, repentance, confession, and admitting that I am a sinner? Those are not bad actions to take; in fact, they are all valuable. However, they are all actions. His presentation of the Gospel plainly included the requirement of good works in exchange for salvation. Since he said salvation is *apart from works* and *a free gift*, it made his presentation self-contradictory.

Words like repent, commit, confess, and turning over your life are flatly in contradiction with salvation being a free gift. A person's decision is only considered commitment if they exhibit physical follow through. Repentance is the stoppage of sin. Confession and admitting are both good works. Turning your life over to the Lord means that you change the way you live. It is deceptive to claim that salvation is a free gift, but will require these types of difficult works. It cannot be both free and costly at the same time.

No amount of theological acrobatics could shake my

strong conviction that there was something wrong with this explanation of the Gospel. I had heard every rationale and explanation. Bible teachers would try to make a distinction between good works *for* salvation and good works *that result from* salvation. Basically, the argument goes something like this: You don't have to do good works to have salvation, but once you have salvation, you automatically will do good works. If you don't, you were never saved in the first place. This was a meaningless distinction. It's like the difference between fast food and a dine-in dinner. For fast food, you pay before you eat, at a dine-in restaurant you pay after you eat. Either way, your dinner has to be paid for. With the descriptions of the Gospel that my professor and everyone else I knew were giving, they claimed that salvation is free because you don't have to pay until after you already have it.

Some might counter by saying, "It's not how many good works you do, but only that you demonstrate *some* good works." That always struck me kind of like those so-called *free gifts* that you hear about on Christian preaching radio. The announcer will say, "As a thank you for your donation of any size we will send you this free gift." It's not a free gift if you have to make a donation to get it. In the same way, eternal life can't be a free gift if I have to behave in order to have it.

I was sick of all of it. I had put so much hope in the seminary and just like every step before, my fragile hopes for theological clarity were dashed to little bits on the hard floor of reality. I had one of those hot angry lumps in my throat as I drove home in my borrowed vehicle. I did not want to leave Christianity behind, but I couldn't see myself continuing along the path I was on. I was tired of pretending that it all made sense. I was agonizing over the inconsistencies. I was sick of acting like it was all so important and meaningful when, in reality, I couldn't even get a basic answer that conformed to the fundamental rules of logic.

For the two hour drive home, I grumbled at God. "What are we supposed to do to be saved?" No tears came as I complained to the creator of the universe. "Lord, why isn't there a coherent answer?" Banging the steering didn't force a reply to my prayers, but it did leave my hand feeling numb.

I didn't officially withdraw from the Seminary, but I never went back either. I suppose I failed evangelism class, but that should come as no surprise. I had been failing evangelism since I was a kid. That was despite the fact that I had worked as a professional evangelist on number of occasions. I had exhausted all my options, and I wanted out. I started looking for the exit door from the ministry.

SHOW BIZ

When I was a high school sophomore, I directed a short film called *Janitor Wars*. It was a spoof of Star Wars set in a high school. Two janitors battle for dominance with mop handles aided by the force. My team and I won the first-place state-wide award. In the years that followed, I had used my graphic design and video skills in the various ministry positions that I held. By the time I had dropped out of seminary, I was ready for a complete change of scenery and occupation. Maybe media would be fun.

For years I had dreamed of becoming a famous speaker and evangelist. Now that that dream was dying a speedy death, I began to transfer my aspirations to a new field. I had been more inspired by movies, especially science fiction and fantasy, than I had by anything which took place in the church for quite some time. I started to envision a new direction for my life.

With what little money I had, I purchased my first video camera. It was a large shoulder mount HDV model. The sizable investment meant that my new plan had better work. I used the network of churches I already knew to book my first summer's worth of video jobs at youth camps. It was an exciting time.

I packed my blue and red jeep, newly refurbished, with all the homemade video equipment I had, buckled my camera into the passenger seat, and hit the road. Monday through Friday, I would make highlight videos of the camper's activities in exchange for a fist full of cash. The summer camps enjoyed my videos, and I enjoyed getting paid. Saturday, I would drive home if I was within a few hundred miles, and Sunday, I would head to the next camp.

I had assumed that I would have enough work to carry me to the end of the summer, but then I'd have to get a *real* job. As summer drew to a close, it was clear that there was plenty of work to be had. From job to job, I was able to keep my camera rolling, always thinking, *after this one, I'll have to get a nine to five.* It never came to that since the video and design jobs kept coming in.

For the previous years, I had been paid minimal coinage, making around $1200 a month by the church. My expenses, like my body, had been skeleton thin. Now things were changing quickly. With every successful production, my income grew along with my reputation. Within months of starting my media business, I was making more money than I ever had in my life. I was not only making a living with a camera, but I was climbing that slippery ladder into the middle class. I called my company Media Kitchen, a clever play on my last name. At the end of the year, my Media Kitchen tax return showed that I had invested 70% of everything I had made that year in new equipment. I was no longer using homemade gear but was filling my small apartment with expensive production gadgets, the likes of which a movie studio could be proud.

It wasn't long before I was able to begin thinking about the kinds of projects I wanted to do. Shooting commercials, training videos, and the occasional TV special for the local channels was enjoyable enough, but I had my eye on a larger prize. I was happy to be making a living, but I wanted to make something else entirely.

My buddy at the time was Tom. We were both unmarried, previous youth ministers, jaded by the church each in our way. Our lives were a constant string of cynical remarks about the nature of Christian American life. We promised one another that if either of us ever got married and had kids, we wouldn't turn out like all the do-nothing yuppies we saw in town.

In light of our enormous portions of free time, Tom and I began to discuss the possibility of making a movie. My desire to be a famous Christian evangelist was now dead and replaced by a more worldly pursuit. My ambition to become a renowned filmmaker had a gravity all it's own. The film we would make began to take shape. Tom would be the principal character, and I would run the camera. We floated scads of ideas before we came to a concept that would change the movie industry forever. The dreamy haze of self-aggrandizement began to tug at me. The illustrious idea was… fortune cookies.

We began to write the script for a modern fantasy we would call Cookie. Actually, I wrote, and Tom read. It was hardly a script, considering that I didn't know the first thing about writing a movie. I had assumed that the writing process was just a formality and that all the magic happens when you finally hit record. For this reason, the story was convoluted, meandering, and ultimately meaningless. Within a few weeks, our script was locked and ready for production.

I knew we would need more people involved in the project if it was going to be any good. I needed some crew to help bring it to life. Tom and I both felt conflicted about this. Managing a large group of people was not my idea of fun. We enjoyed being a duo, but the movie project was snowballing. We'd certainly need some other faces in the movie. It would be incredibly dull if it were an hour and a half of Tom doing meaningless tasks alone.

Tom had been dating a girl from Dallas. She was a smart, well-spoken, and pretty girl. I knew from the time I saw her she'd be great on camera. It wasn't long before we put two and two together. After deliberating on whether their relationship was ready for him to ask a favor, he agreed to give her a call.

After about fifteen minutes of him pacing the front yard with his phone to his ear, and me shadowing his steps trying not to butt into the one side of the conversation I could hear, he hung up. The look on his face didn't betray the outcome.

"She's in." he said. That was that. We had our male and female lead. The next step was to find some crew. We could do it with a crew of two, at the minimum. We'd need at least one more person to pull off our big movie. Unfortunately, my friend list had been whittled down to one, and Tom was already on board. I wasn't sure where we were going to find more warm bodies.

HER

Around that time, I was invited to judge a graphic design project at Kilgore College. My dad had taught advertising and design there for about twenty-five years. He often would invite media professionals to come to the college and critique the student's work. That added a real-world feel to the presentation of the student's design projects. Now that I was officially a *media professional*, I qualified to sit on the panel for critiques. Since judging student presentations usually meant that Dad would buy me lunch afterward, I was happy to do it.

Dad would always introduce the so-called media professionals that were present for the critiques. This time he proudly told his class that I was in production on a movie. He made it sound as if I was in line for an Oscar. I played along, though. In reality, my production was Tom and me alone in a house in the woods. No matter, none of the students would ever know that I wasn't actually awesome. I let Dad brag inaccurately about me, always willing to allow the fictitious version of myself to live on in his head as long as it made him proud.

After introductions were behind us, the students began to present. As was always the case, there were a few that were plain awful. They had no business doing design. I'd struggle to find something positive to say, like, "I find your use of multiple conflicting colors interesting. It really adds tension to the piece." All the while, I'm thinking, *"You need to see an eye doctor because you're clearly color blind?"*

Despite there always being a few that stink, the majority of the projects fell into the category I like to call, "You have potential." Not yet professionals, a large portion of the students had the raw talent that years of grueling work would hone into a usable tool kit of workplace possibilities. Most managed to produce projects that would earn them a solid B+.

What I always looked forward to was the one or two students in every group that stood head and shoulders above the rest. There was always at least one that just had that X factor. It's something you can't teach. Some either have it, the rest don't. You know it when you see it. In a few short years, most of the students who fall into that category would be my competition in the professional world.

That year there were two that stood out as the top tier operators. The first was a man named John. He was at least thirty-five years older than everyone else in the class. I would later learn that he had gone back to school after working as a graphic designer for three decades. He was already a professional, and it showed in his work. He presented with confidence and competence. John spoke not as one trying to get a grade but as one who loved the craft. He had reasons for every color and design choice that appeared in his gorgeous project. I knew with the first look that he would be an A+.

That year there was only one other A+. She had my attention for more than one reason. "Hi, I'm Kristah, and I'd like to welcome you to the future of eyewear," She began as she presented a market-ready piece of advertising. I knew it was good because she made me want to buy those futuristic sunglasses right then and there. Her presentation and design work, like John's, was professional-level quality. She had a clever slogan that got a giggle and had even produced a radio commercial with a professional voice-over actor. Though her work was A+ worthy, I was enamored for another reason. She was super smoking hot.

She wore a white button-up shirt that hugged her attractive lines and a fitted grey skirt. Her professional attire was modest yet classy. Her long golden hair fell past her shoulders and seemed to be ever presently catching a mysterious breeze. She was tall and slender, and it would not have surprised me to discover that she had appeared on the cover of a fashion magazine. She, too, like John, presented with confidence and poise. She was so good and good-looking that I had already decided that if I came into some money, I'd hire her. I knew she wouldn't want to work with a goof like me. She had serious professional potential in her future, but that wouldn't stop me from fantasizing.

After the presentations were all complete, I gave my critique stammering a bit when it came time for me to address Kristah. Her smile was warm as she received my effusive praise. I decided not to ask her to marry me during the critique since that would be showing favoritism to her above the other students. After a few closing remarks from my dad, the class dispersed.

I shook a few hands and congratulated some, including John, on their excellent work. Dad and I walked out to his truck as we chatted about where we would go to lunch. I didn't want to leave yet. I hadn't, however, proposed to my new soul mate. Suddenly I had an idea; I could lie to Dad.

"Where do you want to go for lunch?" Dad asked.

"I think I might have forgotten my phone in the building," I said, even then feeling the weight of it in my pocket. I hopped back out of the truck with a jolt, not acknowledging his question. As I was approaching the tinted glass of the building, Kristah glided gracefully in golden gilded light from the door. She was like a pure sunbeam. *Should I get down on one knee now?* I thought. Instead, I mumbled something nervously.

"Great job on your presentation. It was very professional," I said as I passed by, still pretending as if there was something I had forgotten in the building.

"Thanks," she said as she kept walking. I couldn't believe it; she was totally in love with me. I mean, she hadn't exactly said it in those words, but what else could *thanks* mean? I darted into the building for a few seconds, spun around, pulled my phone from my pocket, and headed back to Dad's truck.

"It was in my pocket the whole time," I said to Dad as I crawled back in his truck. He laughed at my daftness but wasn't surprised. Absent-mindedness was sometimes a convenient character trait. In this case, my mind was far from absent. Finally, answering his lingering question, I called out, "How about Taco Bueno for lunch?"

I watched Kristah walk across the pavement as we pulled out of the parking lot. I wanted to stay, but I was out of lost items. We bumped onto the pavement and began to rumble down the road toward my favorite taco place.

"I think she's the prettiest girl I've ever seen," I said, almost forgetting that someone else was in the truck.

"Amanda?" Dad said. "She's really sweet. She's about to graduate. You know—" I cut him off.

"No, not Amanda!" I responded with a little too much repulsion. I didn't know who this Amanda character was, but I'm sure she was a disgusting gargoyle. In fact, every other woman, but the one I had just beheld, had suddenly and emphatically become uninteresting and unimportant.

"Kristah," I said.

"Oh, yeah," Dad said as if he should have known. "It's neat to have a father and daughter in class together. That's the first time that's happened." What in the curdled milk was he talking about? First, he's trying to chain me to some pseudo-sapian troglodyte named Amanda, and now he's talking about fathers and daughters in his class. He had apparently lost his mind.

"What are you talking about?" I asked.

"You remember the older guy in the class? He had an outstanding presentation."

"John?" I asked.

"Yeah. John is Kristah's dad," he explained.

I couldn't believe it. I had missed my opportunity. I could have asked her dad for permission to marry her and proposed all in one fail swoop. How could I have been so ignorant?

TWILIGHT

It took me two weeks to get up the nerve to send Kristah a message online. I had found her on Facebook the same day but didn't want to seem too eager. It was difficult to wait that long, but it was the obligatory interval for avoiding the appearance of being a creepy stalker.

We had a brief chat in which I attempted my brand of sarcastic humor. I didn't get an LOL, but she didn't seem annoyed either. It was the kind of marginal success that I was willing to accept. After about a five minute chat, we put a pause on the conversation and didn't return to it for a few days. Once again, I didn't want to seem desperately needy, so I left her alone.

Consequently, Friday found me in a positive mood. Tom, who I had spent most of my days with for at least a year, was spending more time with his girlfriend. This meant I was spending more time with myself. I would take long drives down lonely country roads, eat at my favorite fried chicken place, and eventually wind up at the theater. Being single, enamored with movies, and having disposable income was a formula for binge-watching. There were times when I'd see two movies at the theater in one night. Of course, I'd pay for both tickets; I'm not a movie villain. I would also go back to view the same movie a second or third time if it was particularly good.

I'd rarely check what was playing before making my way to the theater, assuming that there was almost always something I could stand to watch. On that particular Friday, there was nothing new that had been released, and I had seen every film that I was interested in. The only thing I hadn't seen was a movie called Twilight. All I knew about it was that it was a vampire love story targeted at teenage girls. The cast was headed by heartthrobs such as Robert Pattinson, Jackson Rathbone, Taylor Lautner, and Kellan Lutz. These exceedingly handsome young men left pubescent girls screaming in theaters throughout the country. I had no idea of the phenomenon that was Twilight. The critics hadn't liked it and you had to forfeit every modicum of masculine dignity to admit you'd watched it, but that was fine. I was bored and wanted to escape my loneliness for a few hours. I had no idea what was in store.

Twilight changed my life. Regardless of whether or not you like the movie, and I did a lot, it touched on something deep. Sure, there were chick flick themes.

There were cheesy parts. Some of the acting was underwhelming. Despite all this, the closing scene left me in this haze of metaphysical longing. Bella and Edward are dancing under the amber glow of their prom night lighting. She wants to be changed into a vampire so that she can be with him forever. She loves him so much that she can't imagine living another day without him. It's a beautiful scene.

I left the theater in a mystical daze. I stood for a very long time in front of the movie poster in the hallway. I'm sure those passing by thought I had experienced a stroke for the long paralysis I seemed to be experiencing. I didn't care what anyone else thought; I was deep in an ethereal trance. I had experienced something. I had been moved. I felt emotion like I hadn't felt in a very long time. I felt what Bella felt. I wanted what she wanted. I don't mean I wanted a pale teen-aged vampire who looked like an underwear model to bite me, but essentially I wanted the same things. I wanted something to care about. I wanted something worth giving my life for. I wanted to be so passionate about something—anything—that it would be worth trading in my ever-loving mortality.

"I wish eternity could feel like that," I whispered. Only the poster could hear me.

"Wait," I said, now fully talking to myself in the hall of the theater. "It will be." The realization smashed into me like a tsunami. Though it was hard to imagine, eternity would be like that, and better.   All the dreariness and mundane effect that had overtaken the church and my faith-life was only a cloud surrounding that which was truly marvelous. Behind the ritual and beyond the ineffectual malaise that had draped itself like a rain-soaked blanket over the world of mortal men and women, there was something deeper and more powerful.

As I scanned the poster, calm on my visible exterior, a gushing wind rose inside my heart. Whatever emotion, passion, or longing that a movie like Twilight produced could only be a thin reflection of the divine experience. For a fleeting moment, I had been touched by something that left an echo ringing in the eternal cavernous depths of my hallow soul. In those brief moments, as I admired the movie poster, the everlasting portion of my spirit cried out. The deep called out to that which is deeper. It was Twilight, of all things, that reminded me what I couldn't stand to live without. Beyond the surface desires, I wanted eternity; I wanted forever. I wanted to be home, finally resting in that grand country beyond the dark sea of confusion and bewilderment. I longed to see what was behind the veil. I wanted the real to reveal itself to my longing soul.

That night I went home and bought the remaining three books in the Twilight series and began to devour them. At certain scenes in the books, I literally shouted aloud at the characters as I read. I went to see Twilight in the theater two more times before its theatrical run was concluded. I didn't miss an opening weekend of the remaining four movies in the series.

The target market for the Twilight series was teenage girls. I was a twenty-five-year-old single man. Addicted wouldn't be a word too strong for how I felt about this piece of fiction. It's for this reason that I did not share my strange infatuation for the story with other adults. Though, it resonated so deeply with me that I had to force myself to stop reading the books for periods long enough to eat, sleep, and do my job.

Twilight had become an anthem for the longing that sat unrequited in the root of my Spirit. I knew that there was something deep and powerful in the Christian experience, but it had somehow escaped my every attempt to capture it. Like vapor in a birdcage, I could never keep the esoteric essence of my faith within the boundaries of my passion for more than a moment at a time. I wanted it back. I wanted to feel a craving for eternity. What Bella felt for Edward, I wanted to feel for heaven, for Christ, and my faith.

INTERN

"I want to admit something, but you can't laugh," I typed. I hadn't seen Kristah since that day in class, but I had a regular line of communication open through facebook messenger. I was careful not to be too friendly, always remembering that she was an eighteen-year-old college kid, and I was in the mid-twenties. It was a caution that had drilled into me during my years working as a youth minister. Often the oldest girls in my youth groups seemed near enough my own age for romance to spark. None the less, they were always irrevocably off-limits. This felt similar.

"I can't promise I won't laugh," she said. "But, I'll try." I smiled as I began to type. I was about to reveal something personal. As of yet, I had played it safe. All through messenger, I had hired her to design a logo for one of my clients and chatted about the details over the last couple of weeks. We had kept it professional and I hadn't yet swerved into that territory where the intimate details of my life were growing. I was about to and it came with the thumping heart of excitement mixed with panic.

"I LOVE the Twilight movie." I stared at the screen for a long moment before I hit send. Was this ok, or would she discover that I was a total maniac? I saw the icon that told me she was typing. I got nervous and began slamming the keys in a flurry of nervous tension. "I know I'm not exactly their target market, but—" I began to write. She beat me to the keystroke.

"WHAT!?!? ARE YOU SERIOUS???" She wrote. This was bad, really bad. She would stop talking to me, hit unfriend, and report me to the police? The hypothetical began to swell in my mind until she deflated my ballooning imagination. "It's my favorite!!! I've seen it eleven times in the theater!" Her messages were coming in fast now. "Twice at the normal theater, then it went to the cheap theater, and you can get a ticket for $0.50 on Tuesday nights."

"Oh, really." A goofy grin was stretching across my teeth now. "You're more of a weirdo than me. I've only seen it three times, but I went and got all the books and read them right after I saw the first film," I typed, before jumping up out of my chair to do a fist pump.

We had broken through the barrier. It seemed now that we were free to eat of any fruit in the garden. We messaged for hours about Twilight fan lore, sequel release dates, and author commentary. She was surprised to find that my knowledge of the books was not a superficial affinity, but a nerd-level fan-boy database. I was surprised to discover that she could match my insider knowledge bit for bit. I begrudgingly admitted that she might love the books *almost* as much as I did, but not more, I was fan number one in the Twilight universe. Obviously, she disagreed, but I was ok with her being wrong on that point.

In the conversation, I told her about my spiritual experience with Twilight. I also explained how Tom and I were working on a movie of our own, called Cookie. She kept her word for the most part and didn't laugh at me, not about Twilight, or at the fact that I was making my own movie. She did laugh at the revelation that I was the number one fan, mistakenly thinking she was first in line for the coveted moniker.

As I went to bed that night, later than usual, I was buzzing with excitement, though I knew that I was hoisting my hopes past the point of reason. With her looks, she could date anyone she liked, and she probably had a boyfriend. That didn't matter anyway since she was eighteen and I was twenty-five. I could not pursue a girl so fresh out of high school, no matter how much I wanted to. That was final. I would go no further. I would have to find a way to stop the infatuation I was secretly nursing.

Not long after that, I got a call from my dad. He was whirring with that characteristic enthusiasm, which swirled around him after a great lecture to a class full of eager students. It was equally likely that he had a cup of caffeine-rich coffee, which always had the same effect. Whatever the case, I could tell he couldn't wait to deliver some news.

"Something interesting happened today," he said, nearly begging me to inquire.

"Oh, did you realize your fly was down during your lecture again?" I asked. He laughed and added.

"I lecture without pants to make sure that never happens. No one falls asleep in lectures anymore." We both giggled like all the adult men in our family were prone to do.

"So, out with it," I said. "What happened?" With the prompt, he took on a tone that I might call hushed. What he was about to say was so tantalizing that he could hardly speak it out at full volume.

"Well, you know that I arrange internships for all of the students in professional practices class." I was fully aware of the class, as he had often spent long hours on the phone with local design agencies pitching and convincing business professionals to take on student interns. It was one of the unique features of his program. It offered the students real-world experience that they could not get within the walls of the college.

"Oh, yeah. Is it intern time already?" I asked, not sure where this was headed.

"Yeah, and the most uncanny thing happened."

"What?"

"There was a student that wanted to talk with me privately after class. She followed me into my office and told me that she wanted to be your intern at Media Kitchen." He allowed a pause to linger, letting it sink in. "Want to know who it was?" He asked, almost like a junior high girl sharing gossip at the lunch table.

"Uh," I said, trying to find a way to tell him that I didn't want an intern. No doubt, it was the ghastly Amanda he had already tried to talk me into dating. I didn't know who Amanda was, but I certainly didn't want to take a chance and have some knuckle-dragging mouth breather staring at me from across my kitchen table as I tried to work. "I'm not really sure I—" He cut me off before I could say it.

"It's Kristah!" he said with a note of triumph as if he had won the gold medal for the international matchmaking championship. "Isn't that weird? Just the other day, you were saying how pretty she is, and now she wants to be your intern, out of the blue."

"Yeah," I said, but didn't want to leave him in the dark. "I mean, I guess it's not entirely out of the blue. I hired her for a logo project a few weeks back," I admitted. I didn't divulge that we'd been talking on messenger about a teeny-bop chick flick ever since.

"You dirty dog," dad said with a laugh, which was quite out of character.

"No, it's not like that. She's just a good designer," trying to get some distance from his implication.

"Well, what do you say? Are you willing to take on your first Media Kitchen intern?" he said with the formal voice he often used as a transition to the official business at hand.

"I don't know. I mean, it's just me and my camera gear here at the house. What would we do?" I said. My mind supplied the answer before dad could respond. *Make out for hours,* I thought.

"Well, she said she's interested in doing a freelance design business just like you. Meet with her a few times. Talk her through your work. Give her a project or two, and that's it. It's easy." He was pouring it on now, thinking I might turn down the opportunity.

My supposed trepidation was false hesitancy. I knew the moment he said her name that I'd do anything to have some alone time with her. I could not resist the opportunity. The fact that she had requested an internship filled me with a hundred kinds of hope.

LAST DAY

The first day of shooting on our movie, which we clumsily called Cookie, just so happened to coincide with the first day of Kristah's internship. The free labor arrived at a perfect time, considering that I needed a film crew. No doubt, it's not what she had expected to be doing for the first day of her college credit co-op, but she worked as our boom mic operator, set dresser, script supervisor, and prop master. She seemed happy to do any seemingly strange task our low budget movie required. She even played the role of a Kung Fu bodyguard in the film.

Both her older brother and sister were theater teachers who directed stage plays for a living. She had often aided them and even played parts in stage plays as early as twelve years old. Her parents were involved in Children's ministry, so she grew up traveling to churches and doing puppets every week. She was no stranger to playing funny characters, creating media, and working on productions of various kinds. She was at home on set and capable of anything I threw at her.

Tom's girlfriend was there as well since she was the other principal actor in the film. The four of us hit it off as if we'd been long-time friends. There was an addictive mixture of accomplishment and fun as we shot what we hoped would be the best movie ever made. The movie would take me another year to complete. I ask you, no, I beg you not to watch it. You can still find it in some dark corner of the internet, but it's not worth the search. I'll tell you why.

There are a few fundamental rules of movie-making, which I didn't know at the time. Some examples include, the main character needs to have a clearly defined goal, and there needs to be an antagonist with an opposing goal. Another rule is, don't foreshadow what you won't fulfill. However, the most essential rule in filmmaking is, never ever let your protagonist murder a dog on purpose. No audience anywhere will continue to root for a canine killer. Ironically, your character can blow holes in human bodies with a shotgun for two hours straight, and people will call it a high-quality action film, but have him shoot one dog, and it is absolute garbage. In fact, if you want your audience to hate a character, all you have to do is have them kill a puppy. The smaller and cuter the puppy is, the more the audience will detest the loathsome perpetrator. Somehow, I missed these rules and consequently broke all of them in my film. No animals were hurt in the actual filming, but the popularity of the movie was pulverized.

Fortunately for Kristah, the entirety of the internship was not consumed by movie-making. When we weren't shooting, Kristah would come to my house for a few hours twice a week. We would talk about business, brainstorm on design and video projects, and discuss how to run the financial books for a freelance design business. She helped me with a few of my commercial video shoots.

She was a bit of an enigma to me. I couldn't calculate why she would want to spend such hours with me. I liked to imagine, as we talked about the bland variety of business-related topics, that we were both holding back a torrent of fiery passion. One sideways glance would begin a crack in the professional veneer, I pretended. It would send us crashing together like two star crossed lovers. It was only a fictional fantasy that I kept hidden from view. If there was any affection on her part, it was not on display. That meant, almost certainly, that she was not interested in my fond regard, but only my professional experience.

As the month was drawing nigh its unwelcomed end, we were scheduled to have one last session. We met in town for the final day of the internship. She rode with her cousin, also a college student at the time. We met up at a sandwich shop with the official goal of a final debriefing. It was meant to be a casual walk-through of the things she had learned. I was supposed to give her a formal critique of her work. We didn't do any of that. She and her cousin were like a jukebox of jokes. They had a half dozen character voices that they performed with each other as they recited funny lines they had accumulated over the last year of living together. They kept me laughing the entire time.

By the time we finished lunch, it was raining like an East Asian Monsoon. Great sheets of water were pounding the parking lot outside. The rain on the roof was the thunderous applause that signaled the curtain was closing on our too few scenes together. The three of us stood at the window, calculating how drenched we would be by the time we each could unlock and enter our respective vehicles. Kristah had ridden with her cousin and was preparing for the inevitable saturation. Seeing as we hadn't done anything in any official capacity, I offered up an option.

"I can give you a ride back to the college. We could do our debrief on the way," I said, trying not to sound needy. With a quick and seemingly knowing glance to her cousin, Kristah agreed. *What did that look mean?*

We got drenched, getting to my car. I turned the engine on to run the heater.

"You'll be appalled at how slow I drive in the rain. I seem to wreck a car every time there's bad weather, so I drive like my grandpa's great-grandma," I said, trying to warm my hands in front of the heater vent.

"It's ok; I don't have any more classes this afternoon."

"Oh, really?" I said, pouring hopefulness into the void that the possibility of an empty schedule created. "Good, because when I said slow, I mean that I leave the car parked until the rain stops." She laughed as she reached toward the vent.

We sat in the front seats for over an hour with the car running and the rain pounded the windshield. The conversation wove through the shadowy enigmas of our childhood memories and the sunny anticipation of the road ahead. The talk unearthed much of what we shared, a starry-eyed wonder at God's love for people, an excitement for life's impossible challenges, and an endless passion for the art and beauty that revealed itself in the mundane moments of life. The relative excitement of a rainy-day chat with a beautiful woman in a confined space amplified the realization that the following day would mark the end of the internship. I would enjoy my time with her as long as it lasted.

"You know what we should do?" she nearly sang out after an hour's conversation in the car. "We should celebrate this incredibly, stupendously, phenomenally successful internship!" I had just been lamenting what a pitiful internship experience I had offered. The other students had trained under grandmasters of advertising industry. She was stuck with me, a self-made ding dong shooting a nonsense movie in his one-room apartment near the woods.

"Well, the celebration should fit the level of success. So maybe we could split a saltine cracker and a half cup of water," I said. Despite the dreary deluge, sunshine was beaming inside the now warm cabin of my car. That was not least in part because she was offering a much-desired extension of our time together.

"It's cheap night at the cheap theater. They're still showing Twilight." I could have gasped aloud. Going to a movie, especially a romantic drama, would definitely blur the lines between professional demeanor and romantic affection. I probably stuttered as I responded.

"That'd b-b-be great!" I said as she smiled back. "I guess we should check movie times," I began to say when she offered them up from memory.

"5:15, 7:00, and 9:20." I looked at her with surprise. "I told you I'm the number one Twilight fan."

"Well played," I said. "How many times—"

"This will be my twelfth time to see it, and I'm still excited." I finally put my car in drive and crept slowly across town in the rain.

It wasn't called the cheap theater for no reason. Movies Nine had been the main attraction in town around the late seventies before it fell into disrepair. It was revitalized in the early nineties, but by the time we walked through the door, it was nearing its long-expected end.

The screen was torn about three-quarters of its height. The ripples from the fabric's scar made Edward and Bella's faces contort in funny ways. There was rainwater leaking; no leaking isn't the right word. There was rainwater cascading through the roof and splattering onto the soaked seats a row ahead of us. Apparently, the fifty-cent movie tickets weren't enough to pay for the heater to turn on because it was like watching a movie from inside an Icee machine.

The entire experience was charming in a way that words can't capture. We quoted along with Edward and Bella as their iconic lines were reproduced through crackling and blown speakers. Even though I was pretty sure this wasn't a date it was the best one I ever had.

FIRST DAY

After the movie, apparently, neither of us was quite ready to say, "good night." The car didn't seem to want to shift into drive as long as the destination was an ending to all that was good in my world. Being a creative duo, it didn't take long for one of us to offer up an alternative to killing the evening's festivities.

"Hey, my cousin's boyfriend is in town," she said after sitting in the car for another few minutes. "They are meeting at Buffalo Wild Wings. We could go get something to eat with them if you like."

I discovered over chicken tenders that her cousin, who was her age, was dating a guy that was my age. What an uncanny coincidence. *Why had her cousin been so adamant in making sure I knew everyone's age at the table?* Was there another knowing glance shared between Kristah and her cousin at that seemingly unsolicited revelation? Notwithstanding, it began to dissolve my fear of the large age gap between us. We ate wings and talked in the dark noisiness of the late-night establishment. She dipped the spicy sauce like a pro; ketchup was the hottest I could handle. Her cousin and boyfriend slipped off into the night after eating, leaving us to continue pretending we were not on a date.

I drove Kristah back as the evening rain began to clear. Piercing moonlight elbowed its way through the clouds, which had hoarded the sky greedily for most of the evening. Though it was no longer raining, I drove slower than needed. Ostensibly for caution, but in unspoken reality, I didn't want the evening to end one second before it had to. My tires were reluctant to pass through the entrance of her college, but I resisted the urge to lap the block. Parting is such a sour sorrow, as they don't say. Climbing out of my car, she gathered her bag and threw the strap over her shoulder. In the open door, she spoke.

"Hey, I need to drive over to Marshall to take my sister a backpack. She's leaving for New York tomorrow, and I told her she could borrow it. I was supposed to get it to her a week ago," she said.

"Oh, ok. Well drive safe," I replied. Finally, she had an excuse to get rid of me. She had played along for most of the evening, probably out of a sanguine pity for a lonely bachelor like myself. No doubt, her time had been offered as a charity, or at best, in thankfulness for the internship. She had been dutiful to sacrifice a few hours in platonic friendship, but now she was ready to rid herself of the chore it was to entertain such a draining counterpart. I wasn't sure how an internship was supposed to end, but I didn't think any of the other employers would have expected a kiss from their interns. I reached for the stick shift preparing to pull out.

"You could come with me if you want," she explained. *I knew it; she's totally in love with me!* I thought. I was getting whiplash from the violent shifts in my internal monologue. I couldn't get the keys out of the ignition fast enough. I would do anything to prolong the *internship,* though it was beginning to feel like we needed to redefine our professional relationship.

"Sure," I said as I killed the car and climbed out. Haley Williams, the lead vocalist of the energetic rock band Paramore was blaring from her speakers when she cranked the car. Their driving rifts, which are the spine-tingling foundation of the Twilight soundtrack, were a welcome familiarity. We oscillated between conversation and listening to our favorite songs as she drove the hour round trip to her sister's and back. I wondered at the relative unimportance of the errand, believing it could be a meaningless task to keep the night alive.

On finally returning to where we had started, I knew this was it. This was the end. There were no more empty errands. It was 3:00 AM on a school night. We had stretched the month-long internship to its maximum, but it was time to say goodbye. A strange mixture of feelings spiraled around me in the few moments that we talked in her car. I didn't want to end it, but I knew it would be inappropriate to continue.

"So, I want to say something," I started. I could feel that familiar lump rising in my throat. I didn't want to fumble this like the handful of dating relationships I had experienced during college.

"What's that?" she said warmly.

"I like you. I don't know if you like me. If you do, I'd like to keep seeing you. If you don't, I think we should not continue, because I've never been good at having female friends." Even as I said it, I could have slapped myself across the face. It seemed so mechanical and rigid. It wasn't how I wanted to sound at all. It sounded like I was reading from a legal document. After a long pause, I tried to clarify. "What I'm saying is, I feel like we should stop now if you don't like me."

"I feel the same way," she said in a pure tone. I had no idea that my entire life had just changed. *What had she said?* That she felt *the same way*, was not good. Now I was regretting my words. *Why hadn't I just left it alone?* Why couldn't I stay in the friend zone, until she realized I was the perfect guy. It was like I had never seen a rom-com before.

"Oh, ok," I said, dejected. I could feel the tender tissue of my paper heart ripping down the middle. I would wait to cry until I got out of her car, but I knew it was coming.

"No, I mean, I feel the same way about you."

"Oh," I said a little baffled. "Oh, you mean—"

"Yeah. I like you too," she explained. "And I appreciate that you're direct about how you feel. So many guys are—"

"Sissy man-children?" I offered in a boastful voice impersonation of Johnny Bravo. We laughed as I took her hand in mine. "Wow, this is unexpected. I totally thought today would be the last time I got to see you."

"I totally hoped it wouldn't be." There was a long silence that followed, but it was the kind of silence that can only exist in the warmly comfortable moments shared by those who are close. We took in the surroundings realizing the world had just changed. I couldn't let it rest, always being the cationarian.

It felt unreal. She was pretty and intelligent. She was funny and profound. She lived by principles but also knew fun. All the cliché stereotypes were shattered in this one amazing eighteen-year-old girl. It seemed too good to be true. Maybe it was. Perhaps I had misunderstood. Maybe I grabbed her hand while having misunderstood. My heart missed a beat at the embarrassment.

"But just to be clear, I'm saying that I want you to be my girlfriend," I blubbered clumsily.

"Yeah, I understand," she said with complete ease.

A KISS

"I don't want our first kiss to be some sloppy slobber job in the parking lot of the Mall," I had said the first week we were dating. "I want it to be somewhere special that's worth remembering." I had enough girlfriends in the past to know that usually, the first kiss is more underwhelming than the movies imply it should be. I was painfully aware that I had kissed other girls, and I could hardly remember with any of them when the first occasion had taken place. Kristah was unique and I didn't want to tumble unintentionally into our first romantic encounter without thought.

"Yeah, let's make it somewhere exotic," she agreed.

"How about underwater?" I offered with enthusiasm.

"I don't think I want to get into a swimming pool in February," she countered.

"We could make out while riding a bike," I tried. We both laughed at the notion. It was creative, but we'd probably both end up toothless and brain-damaged. I tried another, "Maybe in a cave." I knew as soon as I said it that there were no cavers anywhere nearby.

"Maybe up high."

"Yeah, I like it," I said, already knowing what I would do.

I had often spent my afternoons wandering the lonely places among the pine forest my house was cozily nestled against. I usually carried a machete through the foliage, cutting trails in the brush when the path became confounded. I had grown up in the woods, and this was where I felt comfortable. I spent more hours among the trees than I did among people. The trees were quiet in contrast to the noisy thoughtless city. This magical land was where I would stage our romantic rendezvous.

I picked out a tall Texas Live Oak which offered a grand contrast against the more common pines. It shot up against the deep blue sky like a scraper, splitting into two extensive sections about twenty feet up the trunk. The branches above fanned out like the giant skeleton of an umbrella. In the spring, no doubt, it was the image of virility. In the winter months, as it currently was, it had eerie barrenness that somehow attracted me.

Over the next few days, I hauled lumber into the woods behind my house—woods which I didn't own. I am no carpenter, so what I would build would not be a work of constructional genius. It would be simple and unassuming, maybe even a little redneck. I began with steps up the trunk. Next, I would attach pulleys for lifting my supplies. Each day I would gather more materials for the task. Being a grown man, I knew it would seem strange for anyone to see what I was doing. That is why I chose a tree far from sight, but I'm sure the hammer strikes could be heard through the residential properties nearby.

I used an old billboard banner that my brother gave me, probably from one of his advertising agencies' campaigns. It became the roof. An unmatched assortment of boards would be nailed into a zigged floor pattern. It was outfitted with oil torches and a loose set of rails made of yellow nylon rope. To call the thing a treehouse would not be entirely accurate. It was more like a nest for humans in a tall tree.

When it was done, I couldn't wait to bring Kristah to see it. It would be a surprise since I had not told her what I was doing.

When the day finally came, I was sick. It wasn't bubonic bad, but I didn't feel well. Nonetheless, I was too eager to introduce Kristah to our new make out treehouse. Fever notwithstanding, I walked her along the trail that began at my back door. By now, the evening sky was deepening into the dusky shadows of night. I had the torches blazing like little suns in the nascent hopes of the approaching darkness.

She gripped my arm tight when she first laid eyes on what I had done—more precisely—what I had done for her. She knew what it meant. It had been weeks since we had spoken of our desire to make our first kiss memorable. This would be remembered down the corridors of wherever our lives would take us. The amber glow that illuminated the tree haven danced across our faces as I showed her to the first step. Smilingly she glanced down as she ascended the trunk toward the towering treetop perch.

Shortly I followed, not wanting to miss the view. We kissed. True to our wishes, it wasn't a sloppy affair, but classy and appropriate. It was the kind of first worth remembering. We reclined in our treetop home, for a few hours after the sun went down, enjoying the cool breeze. Long after the torches had extinguished and our hands had grown too cold and clumsy for the fine fingered finesse of romantic interplay, we climbed out of the tree and went in.

.

BELIEVE AND FOLLOW

Dating Kristah was unlike any other experience I have ever encountered. Most of the relationships I had with girls had been fraught with uncertainty and unwanted drama. I grew up with only brothers, so the vagaries of the feminine mentality were mysterious. Usually something incomprehensible to me destroyed the relationship. That was not the case with Kristah.

One aspect that was conspicuously absent from the relationship was the entire lack of insecurity. We almost immediately knew where the relationship was going. I know this sounds like an exaggeration, but there was only one thirteen second period in which I feared the relationship might not make it. I was driving in my suburban toward the campus of her college. One fleeting thought waved at me as it passed. It was gone as soon as it came and I'm sure it was just the old habit of relational insecurity crying out as it died in the pure light of a healthy romance.

Other than that one vaporous moment, I knew we would eventually be married. That was a surprise to me. I had become content and even enjoyed living a bachelor's lifestyle. I had often told Tom, "Being single is so good that the girl that could pry me out of it is going to have to be something special." I said this as a 25-year-old single who had determined to save my first sexual intimacy for my hypothetical and future wife. Living a decidedly single life for me meant being a terminal virgin. I was not looking for a wife nor a girlfriend. That's why it surprised me that within a couple of months, Kristah and I were talking about getting hitched.

She met my list of expectations. There was not one single criteria for a wife that Kristah did not both meet and exceed. That was my feeling on the subject, but I would learn later that she had one concern I needed to settle before we could tie the knot.

Her upbringing was similar to mine, save one important detail. She had attended a Bible church as I had, but her church was very, extremely, incredibly adamant about being clear on the details of the Gospel. From the moment an infant finds themselves in the nursery and all through the ministries of Cypress Valley Bible Church, where she grew up, there is a consistent focus on clarifying, stating, and reiterating the saving message of Jesus. Conversely, her church made it their goal to remove all of the unneeded complexity and confusion that surrounds most presentations of the Gospel. She was clear on what the saving message was but simultaneously knew that many people were not. She came of age in this fundamental truth, and it characterized her down to her every molecule.

That being her childhood, she knew the kind of friction it would cause to marry someone who was not clear on the Gospel or opposed her church's common-sense method of explaining it. She knew at some point she would have to talk with me about all this, but she is a gentle soul who avoids confrontation when possible. She needed to be certain that I knew what the saving message is, but was cautious in approaching the subject, knowing that it can be a very divisive topic.

"How long are you staying there?" I asked over the phone. She was in Vidor, a town near the Texas coast where the humidity is as thick as it is sticky. Her mother's side of the family lived in that area and she visited often.

"Just through the weekend," she said. I was sitting under the bunk bed in my one-room apartment. I stared up at the underside of the mattress as I lay lazily across my fluffy blue couch. We talked on the phone for the better part of the night. I still hadn't moved beyond the excitement of late-night calls. It was soothing to talk before bed, an experience I hadn't had since sharing a room with my brother in the third grade. On many occasions, we would leave the phones on speaker as we fell asleep. The digitized sound of breathing coming through the tiny phone speaker was comforting somehow.

"Ok, well, if you're not back by Monday, I'll know what that means," I said.

"What will that mean?"

"You've fallen for a Columbian lover named Santiago Sánchez, and have been swept away to his South American estate to work the plantation's cocoa fields," I explained with a straight face.

"I'm sure you'll rescue me if that happens," she said before we both laughed. We could go on for hours with these kinds of imaginary scenarios. The conversation would oscillate between the fantastical and the practical. The cycle had circled in this way for most of the night. So it was not unexpected that she would follow this humorous fiction with a serious inquiry. I would not know until years later, how pivotal the coming moment would be.

"How do you present the Gospel?" she asked casually. She was a better actor than I had known since so much was riding on that question. I didn't realize it at the time, but her father, John, had recently been forced out of a missionary organization. He had worked there for decades before being asked to quit. It was all because he disagreed with the Calvinist leadership about the content of the Gospel. So the wound was still fresh. She knew what kind of tension a Gospel disagreement could cause.

Not knowing any of this, I began to answer the question with all the academic credentials that followed my name. I thought of myself as a bit of an expert in the Bible, notwithstanding my various confusions that I kept to myself. When I didn't know the answer to a question, I would be long-winded. That had always worked in the past, and I was sure she would be impressed with my extensive Bible knowledge.

"How do I present the Gospel?" I repeated. "Ok, well, it all begins in the Garden of Eden." That's right; I began my so-called Gospel presentation in the garden. I talked about the fall of man, the flood, the Jewish law, the nation of Israel, the coming of Christ, his death and resurrection, and his promise to return. I iterated that Jesus had died on the cross for the sins of the world and that he offers salvation. I repeated phrases that I'd heard from Bible teachers and professors like commit, confess, repent, faith, follow, and about a dozen others.

I wove a factual sounding threadwork of Christian clichés that was sure to awe. I talked just long enough to convince her that I knew every inch of the Biblical narrative. When I finally shut my mouth, I expected her to express her admiration for my thorough approach. I honestly expected her to be impressed by my depth and breadth.

She, however, saw right through all of the hocus-pocus of my theological sleight of hand. She had never been confrontational with me, nor had she ever disagreed with anything I'd said, so what followed was like a punch in the stomach, but with a velvet boxing glove.

"I think it's much more simple than all that," she said as if she were tiptoeing across thawing paper-thin ice. A knot twisted in my stomach. She caught me. This eighteen-year-old girl had unmasked my sophisticated attempt at obfuscation. She had peered beyond my convoluted presentation and seen what lay at the center of my Gospel knowledge, nothing but a rocky core of confounded misunderstanding. I was in the same moment embarrassed and intrigued. I betrayed no hint of the contradiction now floating in equal buoyancy in my mind.

"What do you mean?"

"There is a difference between a believer and a follower of Jesus," she said as if it were as plain as the noonday sun. The revelatory utterance was commonplace for her. She had come up in this understanding and it seemed entirely natural. She was aware that some did not see or even understand the distinction, but she hoped I would be open-minded enough to consider it.

For me, it was like the ground shifted beneath my feet. I darted up from the couch. Now I was pacing back and forth. My legs acted as auxiliary pumps that gushed the oxygenated blood to my brain.

"Hmm, that's interesting," I said as if it were only a slight adjustment, only a few degrees difference from the presentation I had just given, though I knew it was fundamentally foreign. It was set apart from anything I had ever conceived.

I had grown up in a   Bible church, gone to Bible college, and some seminary. I had been a minister and an avid listener to thousands of sermons. With all of that Bible focus, I had never heard anyone so much as imply that believing in Jesus and following Jesus was separate. I had learned and hardily believed that having faith in Christ meant that you would automatically follow him thereafter. The implication was clear and challenging to harmonize with Scripture. If a person had truly believed, according to my former mindset, they would inevitably reshape their lifestyle to match their new faith. It, however, had caused all kinds of practical obstacles. If someone necessarily has to follow Christ after receiving salvation, and following Christ equals behavior, then wouldn't that mean that we are being saved by doing good works? That puzzle had produced a preponderance of confusion for me.

Now, this young girl had a compelling answer. I was not convinced at that moment, as much as stimulated. I was a hound dog on a new scent. I knew I would have to chase this trail to see where it led. Could it be that this was the answer for which I had been searching?

CHASING MIST

Kristah and I had been dating for a while when she asked me to join her for a Bible conference in Dallas. It was the annual meeting of the Grace Evangelical Society. I had never heard of the group, but I would later come to find out that they are an organization that has spent decades helping people just like me find clarity on what the Bible says about salvation and discipleship.

"Tony Evans will be there," she explained. This was a massive draw for me. I had grown up listening to Dr. Evan's national radio show. I had always enjoyed his intelligent delivery. Once when I was in college, I had visited his enormous church in the Dallas area. I attended with a few friends from Africa who lived in my dorm. Finding out that Dr. Evans was a regular speaker for the GES conference offered legitimacy and credibility in my mind. All of the other speakers on the schedule were unknown to me. But she promised Tony, so I promised to go.

Dr. Evans' talk came early in the day. I enjoyed it. He was dynamic and powerful in his delivery. I saw nothing unconventional about his talk, but these unknown guys that followed him—wow! They were saying some of the most intriguing things. It was as if they were *really* reading the Bible and following the text wherever it led, even if it ended in unconventional places. I found it incredibly exciting. There was talk of glorified bodies, the outer darkness, the judgment seat of Christ, and eternal rewards. It was all terribly fascinating.

In the afternoon, a tall frenetic man with infectious energy skipped to the front of the room. I glanced at the schedule and found his name quickly. Dr. Robert Wilkin. I'd never heard of him, but he was going to tell us something about the letter of first John. He wove together an exciting talk. It wasn't even the main point, but he commented about what it means to love Jesus. At his words, I recognized a division happening in my mind. Without knowing he was doing it, Dr. Wilkin severed that connection in my brain with the exacting precision of a surgeon.

Dr. Wilkin showed convincingly that to *love Jesus* means to obey his commandments. That was no conjecture. It's actually a direct quote from Jesus. He then pointed out that we are not saved by following the commandments but by having faith. Also, that's not opinion; it's precisely what the Apostle Paul said. Dr.

Wilkin then made the simple conclusion that *loving Jesus* is not the same thing as saving faith and therefore, not a requirement for gaining eternal life.

This commitment to philosophical and theological clarity was immensely refreshing. The evangelists I had listened to for the previous years would say that you need to "love Jesus to be saved." They would then follow it by saying, "Love isn't an emotion; it has to do with how you live." This was clearly contradictory to the notion that we are saved apart from works. To me, it was crucial. The dead ruins of my theological past suddenly began to reassemble themselves. This was the kind of logic I had wanted to see pastors, evangelists, and Bible teachers apply to scripture all my life. I had never heard anyone who was this committed to being logically and Biblically consistent.

As soon as his talk was over, I couldn't wait to get to the front of the room. He glanced up as I barreled forward. I asked him a simple question.

"Can someone believe in Jesus and not love Him?" I asked as if the roof would fall in at any moment.

"Sure," he said as he gathered his notes from the talk. "There's a difference between believing in Jesus and being a follower of Jesus." He gave a quick explanation from various verses. It was beautiful in its simplicity, but monolithic in its importance.

After a quick, "thank you," I wandered out of the convention hall, leaving Kristah behind without an explanation.

There was a small courtyard outside where I found myself, pen in hand, a few moments later. I could feel the gravity of the moment. I wanted to write down what I had just discovered. I began to scribble on the page when I realized that it wasn't only ink that wet the surface. Tears, real fat splattering tears began to fall on the page. I sensed that this was a storm, not a quick spring shower. I arose quickly and began to look for the nearest bathroom.

I wasn't sure if I was going to throw up, huddle on the floor in the fetal position, or just stare into the mirror and try to remember my name. I found my way into the nearest stall and locked it. For the next ten minutes, I cried like a baby—a baby who just realized his high priced theological education was skewed and misinformed. I thought of all the people that I had taught over the past ten years, people who I had told lies to without even knowing it. I had said things I was now ashamed of.

You should know there are only two things that can make me cry: a perfect Muchaco® from Taco Bueno and sound theology. I've never encountered the former, but I had been in the presence of the latter and it left the waterworks running.

It felt as if my understanding of the Bible was an engine that had seized up and been rusted out for years. With this new set of ideas in place, it was as if that engine suddenly was running again. It wasn't just running; it was roaring. It had power and torque. I quickly began ramping the throttle in my mind.

I ran through verse after verse as I stood teary-eyed next to the toilet. Dozens of passages that I had studied for the past 20 years slid together like a working gearbox. I had been grinding the gears so long, I had forgotten what it felt like for things to make sense. I had lived in the so-called mystery that I had forgotten the prismatic beauty of understanding.

The simple explanation that my father had given when I was six was right. Eternal life comes by faith alone. What I had gotten confused was that discipleship comes by hard work, and is not automatic. With this new basic understanding, the Bible came alive in a way that it never had before, or at least in a way that I hadn't experienced since I was a child.

Kristah wondered why my eyes were red when I returned to her. Five minutes of the next talk had already passed, but I didn't mind coming in late. My loving girlfriend looked into my red, teary bloodshot eyes with genuine concern. I silently mouthed the words, "I'll explain later." Then added, "They're good tears."

This gave me a lot to think about on the ride home and over the next few weeks. On my arrival back, I wrote a letter to one of my favorite Bible professors from my university days. Here's what I said:

* * *

Hello Dr. Sterling. This is Lucas Kitchen. I have had an interesting experience that I wanted to tell you about. Over the last few years, I have heard myself saying things like: Grace is free, but if you don't have fruit in your life, then you probably didn't believe in the first place. I recently attended a GES (Grace Evangelical Society) conference. One of the things that was discussed was the absolutely free nature of grace—that one does not need to have fruit to gain eternal life. Fruit is related to eternal rewards instead of eternal salvation. I was more clear on this point when I was young as far as I can remember, but in the last few years, I feel like I had gotten away from this thinking unknowingly. After a very emotional experience at the conference, I feel like I have found my feet again like I've come home for the first time in years. It's as if I've been chasing vapor only to discover that hidden by the mist is this entire kingdom that I once knew about but forgotten existed. I feel like I understand anew what is so amazing about grace. This is the first time that I've been emotionally moved about something theological in years. I had let some really nasty thinking creep into my theology. Namely legalism. I really want to work through this so that I can begin to share this wonderful re-discovery of grace with people. I look forward to hearing from you. -LK

I never heard a response from him. I even tried calling his office, but he wasn't there. Nonetheless, I'm glad I wrote him this note, because it is a time capsule that reminds me what I was feeling and thinking around that time.

My entire world had changed in a matter of

moments. My life was moving in a new direction. I could not wait to tell other people. I had found the clarity I was looking for and I wanted others to find it as well. I prepared to bring others in on the truth.

CLARIFY

"Have you ever heard of free grace theology?" I asked my friend Teddy. Free grace was what I had learned to call the theological outlook which I had now adopted. I was finding it difficult to explain to my old friends what my new perspective was. Teddy was a pastor in his late fifties. He ministered at a local but sizable baptist church. At my question, he furrowed his eyebrows and looked to the ceiling.

"I don't think so. Why do you ask?" he said.

"My fiancé goes to a Bible church where they teach free grace theology. It's neither Calvinism nor Arminianism. It's fascinating," I said. Teddy leaned in, always eager for those rare theological conversations. He had just received his Ph.D. and seemed to be interested. I was ready to try to explain my new understanding of the Gospel. I was excited, thinking it would be as simple as tipping over dominos.

"Give me the overview. What's free grace all about?" he said. It was a little jarring to realize that a long-time pastor with a Ph.D. in theology had never even heard of this brand of Biblical interpretation.

"The basic premise is that there is a difference between a believer and a follower. To be saved, you simply have to believe in Jesus, but becoming a follower is not automatic. It's possible to get saved but then do nothing of spiritual value afterward." I said this suspecting I probably wasn't explaining it quite right. Even as the words came out, they didn't feel complete. The look on Teddy's face let me know that it was not only unfamiliar but that it didn't compute. I resisted the urge to try for more explanation as he considered his response.

"I don't know. It seems to me that one of the things the church has failed to understand is the corporate nature of the salvific narrative. Salvation, although applicable to the individual when appropriated by faith, is experienced corporately by the bride of Christ as a whole," he said. He seemed to think that he was talking about the same thing as I was, though I could not see how that had anything to do with what I had said. I tried again.

"I've often heard 'someone who is *really* saved will inevitably bear fruit,' which means doing good works. I've also heard 'If there's no fruit, there's no root.' Free grace claims that is not true. Grace theology says that believers *should* bear fruit but that it's not automatic. Have you ever encountered that idea?" I asked. At this point, I was no longer trying to convince him, but just trying to explain the position. Teddy took a deep breath. He looked like he was tracking with me this time.

"I see what you're saying," Teddy responded. Now it was me that leaned in thinking we were getting somewhere. "The problem with a lot of Christians is that they do not realize that this whole thing is not about ritualistic religion; it's relational and experiential." He went on for another minute or two, discussing the various misunderstandings that others experience. As far as I could tell, it didn't have anything to do with what I was discussing. It felt like an avoidance mechanism more than an attempt to answer my genuine inquiry. I tried once again.

"It's the idea that salvation is completely free to those who have faith alone in Christ alone. On that, most evangelicals agree. Where the debate rests is upon whether or not a person can really have assurance. If I have to persevere until the end of my life to know that I'm saved, then I can't know if I'm *truly* and *finally* saved until I'm dead. However, First John says that I can *know* that—" He cut me off this time.

"Ahh, that's a good point. I see where you're going with this, and I can't say that I disagree," he said. I was relieved. We had finally landed on the same page. I listened as he laid out his opinion on the matter, or so I thought. "It's similar to the mystery of the hypostatic union, the trinity, or transubstantiation for catholics.

These are divine mysteries that we should take joy in, even celebrate. We can embrace the mysteries of God and love Him more for them. It's in His immense mystery that we realize his incredible sovereignty."

"So, how are your kids doing these days," I asked. I was done trying to get answers from him. Appealing to divine mystery was an old tired trope I had seen plenty of times. When a question arises that a pastor or teacher can't answer, rather than merely saying, "I don't know." they will pontificate on the sovereign mysterious depths of God. Obviously, there are plenty of mysteries concerning God, but I was quite sure that the requirements for salvation could not be a mystery, or no one could get saved. I could see I would not find answers with this Ph.D.

In the following weeks and months, I would receive many blank stares, befuddling responses, and irritated rebuttals. It was as if I had found a pearl of high price, but every time I showed it off to someone, they scoffed as if it were only a discarded clod of mud. My failure to communicate reached its apex a few months later, when I decided it was time to go public.

REJECTED

Although I had officially exited vocational ministry a few years earlier, I still occasionally received invitations to speak at church-sponsored events. In the south, there is a tradition called 'See You At The Pole.' Christian students gather around the flag pole of their school and pray for their friends, teachers, and a host of other related topics. It's a way to show solidarity among young believers.

I suppose the church felt left out of this practice because only a few years after the ritual began, youth groups started having corresponding rallies either the night before or the night after. They are called 'See You At The Pole Rallies.' One of these rallies usually included a worship band and a speaker. I was invited to speak at one such rally, which was to happen at a very familiar place.

Red Oak Fellowship was hosting the city-wide rally for their town. I had often spoken there. It was the location of the dubious question and answer session a couple of years earlier. With my fresh understanding of the Gospel, I viewed my previous statements made from that very stage with infamy. I was still ashamed of the things I had formerly preach at Red Oak Fellowship, and I saw this as my opportunity to make right what I had taught so wrongly.

The room began to fill with enthusiastic teens a little after six. I was always excited to speak for any event of any size, but this night offered an extra measure of butterflies. I knew what I was going to talk about might be considered controversial at this eclectic meeting. That was in part because churches from all over town and a dozen different denominations were joining the night's festivities. What was expected of me was an ecumenical message that could work for Baptist, Methodist, Presbyterian, and Catholic students. What I had planned to speak on would be the most divisive and controversial message I had ever shared.

The night began well. My buddy, who had invited me, led the music. The kids were excited to be in a rally with so many of their friends from school. After the band ramped the energy level in the room to astronomical heights, I approached the stage.

From my first line until my closing remarks, the message was unconventional. I shared a handful of stories about how I had been confused for years about the saving message of Jesus. I talked about the overwhelming frustration I had experienced in my search for answers from church leaders. The audience was engaged as I yarned about my decision to leave the ministry and pursue a different life goal because of my debilitating bewilderment concerning salvation.

All of this was a great set up. I had planted the question in their minds, and now they wanted to know, "What's the answer?" This is where it began to come off the rails. In retrospect, I know now that I was not ready to speak intelligibly about grace. I had rearranged so many of my views on salvation that I wasn't really ready to give a convincing explanation.

I tried and failed to clearly explain the difference between having saving faith in Christ and loving Him. I attempted to make sense of the free grace perspective to an unfamiliar crowd of teens and youth ministers in my remaining five minutes. It was a disaster. What I said to that crowd was not only new, but it was met as if it were spoken from Hell's own heretic.

After I finished, I witnessed the worst thing an event speaker can. My buddy, the minister who had invited me, had a group of other youth ministers circled up around him. They looked angry, and they were letting him have it. I couldn't hear the conversation, but I knew it wasn't good.

"What was that about?" I asked my friend after they had exited the building in a huff.

"They're mad," he said.

"At what?" I asked.

"At you. They are under the impression that you told their youth that they don't have to love Jesus." He paused. "Did you say that?" he asked.

"You heard what I said didn't you," I countered.

"No, I didn't. I had to step out of the room for a minute. When I came back, these guys cornered me and told me you don't want people to love Jesus."

"I didn't say they shouldn't love Jesus; I said that's not the same thing as saving faith. It's not the same thing as believing in him for salvation. Everyone should love Jesus, but it's not what gets you into heaven," I said. Certainly, he'd see that this was just a misunderstanding.

"Yeah, that's what they said you told them," he said. Our relationship was never quite the same after that night. It was my new understanding of *faith alone* which put that friendship in jeopardy. I still talk to him from time to time, but the closeness we had shared began to dissolve. Suddenly Jesus' words began to make more sense. "I have come to turn a man against his father, a daughter against her mother." My buddy and I had been more than friends. For years we had been like family. Now we were being divided. It was the circumstances that were tearing us apart, but those circumstances were born out of my view of the Gospel.

I suppose word travels fast because I did not receive any more invitations to speak at Red Oak Fellowship or any other church. In fact, I didn't speak to another crowd about Christ for years.

It was for the best. Certainly, the divide was inevitable, but I had also learned an important lesson. Don't speak about a subject, especially a new subject, until you're ready to defend it. I was utterly convinced of the truth of the free grace message, but I was as of yet unable to handle the questions that come.

IMPROVE

As the invitations to speak dried up, I began to realize that I needed the break. I had to gather my thoughts and reconsider everything. It was brash of me to think that I was ready to talk publicly about something so new to me. There were dozens, maybe hundreds of questions that I needed to consider.

In the year that followed, I began to realize how disheveled my life had become. It was like coming out of the tornado shelter after a terrible storm to discover that everything is in shambles. I had allowed some horrible habits to take over my life. Thousands in credit card debt was hanging from my neck. All my spending habits were all about me. I was selfish with my money and my time. I was bitter at church and had stopped attending anywhere with regularity. I didn't pray anymore because I couldn't see the point. I was embarrassed to identify as a Christian publicly, and when the subject came up, I would dodge it with obtuse reclassifications that would hide my beliefs. I had become unforgiving and grumbled about people behind their backs. I hated anyone that wasn't like me. I felt defensive around anyone that was like me. I cussed like a dock worker, and I looked at porn all the time. Of course, I hid my habit from the audiences I spoke to in previous years, but now that I was no longer in ministry of any kind, I couldn't pretend that things were beautiful.

The legalistic bubble I had lived in had offered me no help in any of these areas. The legalistic view of the Gospel kept driving me deeper into the sins I was now drowning in. In a community of legalists, you have to pretend your sin doesn't exist, or at least that your failures are only an occasional exception to your otherwise glorious lifestyle. I had become convinced that there was no hope of ever escaping the icy grip of pornography, and could hardly recognize the other more subtle sins in which I was engaged.

Legalistic pastors like Chan, Piper, Washer, Chandler, and MacArthur, had taught me that everyone fails *sometimes* and that we are all sinners. Though if you get *too* deep into sin, then you're probably not saved, according to them. Since my sins were not as bad as many other people, according to the legalist's teaching, I was still saved. I didn't fear that I would be thrown into hell because I knew how much better I was than other people. It's embarrassing even to write that. I had unwittingly signed the legalist manifesto, and it turned me into an unmitigated judgmental jerk.

I didn't think I was in danger of hell, so I couldn't see any incentive to getting clean. If I have salvation, why should I stop using porn? I had rationalized pornography and created ingenious sounding reasonings that justified my disgusting habits. Blaming others for my bitterness and hatred was my method. I soothed the frustration with my selfish spending habits. I was in a mess. Until I came face to face with grace, I didn't even realize how much destruction I had caused in my own life.

It was the legalism of both Calvinism and Arminianism that had led me to the most unhealthy spiritual place I had ever been. It was Lordship salvation, the teaching that we must obey Jesus to get saved, that landed me in the cesspool of sins that I now sat. Trying to be good enough to be saved meant that I held the measuring stick up to other people, and I saw I was in better shape than them. That allowed me to happily retain a handful of sins in my life, thinking that I was doing pretty well comparatively. Once grace reentered my life, I knew I needed a fix, and I wasn't sure how to make it happen.

Despite all of this mess, Kristah loved me. She knew I had some problems that needed some work, but we had spoken often of my new understanding of the Gospel of grace. Having the assurance of someone's love does amazing things both in physical and spiritual life. I knew Christ had saved me on one condition: my faith in Him to do so. That offered me a rock-solid foundation on which I could begin to rebuild my life. I also knew Kristah loved me and would be patient with me as I worked through these debilitating issues.

The first thing I began to work on was my debt. I wanted to marry Kristah, but I didn't want to enter into the marriage with a bunch of credit card interest payments around my neck. I felt like I should pay it all off before we got married. I knew it wouldn't be fair to her to have to pay for my frivolous and selfish pre-marriage spending.

I also knew that living the life of a single man for so many years meant I had several habits that I needed to eradicate. Pornography was the obvious culprit. It had to stop, but I was confident it would not be easy.

"I look at porn sometimes," I told Kristah one sunny afternoon as we sat behind my house. What better way to ruin a get together with your girlfriend than to talk about looking at other women naked? I was nervous for her to know, but I wanted to make things right. It wouldn't be fair for us to continue our relationship with her in the dark about my hidden habit.

"Really?" she said. It was simple, but betrayed no emotion.

"You know how some people say, 'I struggle with it,' when in reality they are not struggling so much as deliberately swimming in it?" I said.

"Yeah," she responded with a slight laugh.

"Well, there are certainly times I'm swimming in it," I said before pausing. I thought it was going to be harder to talk to her about this than it was. I had turned it into a monumental concern when, in reality, she handled it like everything else, with grace and poise.

"Are you swimming in it now?"

"I guess you could say, I'm looking for a path out of the pool," I explained but then added. "I've had some success lately."

"That's good. I'm proud of you!" she said enthusiastically. There was no scorn or condemnation. I knew she would continue to love me, whether I was winning or losing. With a smile, she added, "Let me know if I can help in any way."

It was as simple as that. We had had the porn talk, and it went surprisingly well. Unfortunately, I did not accept her help at that time. My pride and ego was still a thing of legend. It was yet another thing that needed work. The temporary victories I had over porn were enough to keep me hopeful that it would all go away on its own if we got married. I foolishly thought that from the wedding night onward, I would never struggle with porn again. What an idiot I was.

ENGAGED

"You want to come over tomorrow?" I asked Kristah on the phone.

"Sure," she said happily.

"Ok. Bring shoes and jeans, because I want to show you the new trail I cut in the woods," I said as if it were just another of my bizarre projects born of long hours alone in among the pine trees.

The day came finally. I was jittery with excitement. I grabbed my twelve-gauge shotgun, just in case we encountered wild hogs. I knew they were in the area because my yard was constantly getting rooted up. Kristah arrived a little after lunch. It had rained in the morning, and the temperature was perfect for an outside hike. The clouds draped across the sky like a bolt of sheer fabric.

She followed me, machete on my hip and gun in my hand, as we wove our way through the woods. Having a girlfriend who enjoyed the outdoors was never a must, but it was a fantastic bonus. She had grown up camping and canoeing with her dad. She was as alive among the trees as I had ever been. I took us on a circuitous route, about a half-hour circle, before I brought her to the mouth of my new trail.

"This is Butterfly Trail," I said proudly. I had named it for a curious companion that followed me as I cut a swath through the forest. The opening of the path yawned wide. She smiled as we entered the narrow corridor. Sunbeam spires pierced the gaps in the canopy above. The trail snaked through a vine-covered pass and under a thick blanket of green. The path, which had taken me days to complete, was only a short walk that crested the nearest hill before descending back downward into a grassy valley. It opened up into a clearing, not so different than the one Edward and Bella had found in Twilight. That wasn't my intention, but it was a bonus.

As we stepped into the lonesome meadow, the breeze tickled the grass at our ankles. She noticed the two pillars almost at once. Jutting up from the ground, about as tall as I was, were two large wooden spires. On top of each was something of importance. On the pinnacle of the closest pillar was a love letter. It had the look of age as if it were an ancient letter of a long-forgotten time. It was written in my hand, confessing what she already knew. I had fallen irrevocably and unconditionally in love with her. She cried as she read it.

The second pillar had upon it, a small treasure box. We sat on a blanket as I handed her the treasure box. Her eyes widened as she opened it. Within, she found three rings mounted in a slot cut into a strip of leather. Above each ring was written one word, Faith, Hope, and Love, respectively. Below the rings, there was another aged note. This is what it read:

> *Each of these three rings represents something special.*
>
> *Faith: My parents got this ring when I was born. For me, this ring represents the faith that we both found at a young age. Like a child, we follow in that way.*
>
> *Hope: This is the ring I have worn since I was 13 years old to show my commitment to be abstinent and wait for marriage. This whole idea was based on the hope that someday I would find someone to love, and I have that now.*
>
> *Love: this is the wedding ring that your grandmother wore for half a century because of how she loved the man she married. Now I'd like you to wear it for the man you will marry.*

After her eyes left the note and came to my face, filled with tears I reached for the box. I removed the engagement ring and spoke the most romantic words you'll ever hear.

"Which finger is this supposed to go on?" I said. She laughed and slapped at me playfully. "Seriously, though. Which finger." She put out her hand as I said, "Kristah, will you marry me?"

"Yes," she said.

We laid on a blanket in the tall dancing grass, watching the sky's parade of white and blue. The clouds were an apt metaphor for everything I had experienced. The floating effervescence signified myriad mysteries that had vexed my soul for most of my life. What had only been enigmatic shapes against the deep indigo expanse had materialized into substance and meaning. The floating designs in the sky weren't amorphous bodies any longer. They spoke a story as old as the mountains and more ancient still. They poured out purpose, like rain, upon the earth. I had come to think the truths of God were like the clouds, subjective and nebulous, their form being open to any interpretation one desires to give. It was the woman lying by my side who helped me to see the fluffy shapes for what they are. We were suspended in a perfect moment, as sweet as the intermittent sunshine that warmed our skin. It wasn't long before I invented an impromptu plan to heighten the romance.

"Hey, we should start this thing off with a bang!" I nearly shouted with the glee of the moment. "Would you like to shoot my gun?" I was accordingly excited about my brilliant and romantic idea. She didn't seem so impressed.

"Uhh, I don't know."

"Come on; it'll be great!" I said, not realizing that everyone did not share my Robinson Crusoe lifestyle. The things that excited me, the forest hermit, were not quite the same things that one does on their engagement day. Eventually, she agreed.

She took the massive gun to her shoulder and slowly squeezed the trigger. The impact kicked her back so hard that I'm quite certain she would have fallen to the ground if it had not sent her sprawling backward into my chest. I took the gun back as she rubbed her aching shoulder. She has not pulled the trigger on another firearm since.

Before we left the meadow, she began gathering flowers to dry and use for decorations in the ceremony. By the time we got back to my house, she had picked out a date for the wedding. Things began to move quickly from that point.

It wasn't long before we bought a house in Longview, the town where she lived. I took up residence as soon as the title was signed. She still lived at her parent's house and would move in after the wedding. No funny business, of course, we were both still virgins.

She found a beautiful Spanish style villa outside of town where we could have a bohemian ceremony and reception. The wedding was quickly rushing toward us. Life was twisting and turning in new ways.

MARRIED

My wedding day began with me and my dad stealing a truckload of bamboo. Kristah wanted an arbor of greenery that we could stand under for the ceremony. Like always, I had waited until the last moment.

"There's some!" I shouted as we rolled down the road in Dad's truck. I hopped out, machete in hand, and began to slice at it like a chef set loose on grand stalks of celery. The bamboo robbery went unnoticed by the police. When my grandmother saw the arbor, my dad and I constructed, she said, "I just don't know why you'd want to stand under a bunch of dead sticks." Leave it to Granny-Ma to say precisely what she thought.

The wedding was in the middle of May. My wife says we got married on the fifteenth, but I'm pretty sure it was the tenth. The scene was set beautifully at Hunt Villa, dead sticks, and all. The Spanish style mansion that we rented filled with the aroma of Asian cuisine.

Kristah's friend, Patra, owned Little Thai House downtown, so we hired her, a local legend of a chef from Thailand, to cook a wondrous assortment of Pad Thai: pineapple fried rice, chicken larb, and spring rolls for the reception. The gourmet meal was consumed in great heaping portions with much appreciation and awe.

I wrote my vows sitting on a rope swing in front of the mansion. Kristah and I had been apart for most of the day, longer than we had in weeks. The hanging swing was the location at which I would get my first glimpse of my bride to be. She snuck up behind me, though I knew she was coming for the entourage that follows a bride about on the big day. Her flowing dress glided across the grass gracefully. Her wedding gown hugged her attractive lines before billowing outward around her knees. Her stylist had drawn her hair back in an arrangement worthy of a princess at a ball. She was the vision of beauty and grace.

We kissed gently, trying not to communicate her red lipstick to my makeup-less face. The supposed privacy of the seminal moment was artificial since a half dozen of her wedding party and a photographer were lurking nearby. I found it incredibly awkward for the photographer to call out, "kiss her again!" I played along, not minding the kiss itself.

"This time tomorrow, we'll be on a boat to the Bahamas," she said, trying to see past the busyness of the anticipated day. For our honeymoon, we were taking a Caribbean cruise.

"Yeah, but we have to do one thing first," I said.

"What?" she asked, knowing it was unlikely to be serious.

"We've got to lose all these Peeping Toms. I was thinking we could elope. We could head down to the Justice of the Peace. You already have a white dress on."

"You're not going to get out of this that easy," she said with a smile. Transitioning smoothly to the administrative tasks every bride must balance, she added, "do you have down what you're going to say?" I held up my little notebook. I had just finished writing before she arrived.

I had been available but absent-minded during the planning of the wedding. Kristah would call on me for indifferent decisiveness when two shades of purple were proving too obstinate to choose between. I had never envisioned my wedding day, and therefore would be easily pleased by the occasion. There was, however, one thing that Kristah and I both wanted to have as part of our ceremony. Months earlier, we had concocted the scheme.

"You know what would be cool," she had said with her wedding planning book spread out in front of her, along with a dozen fabric samples splayed across the kitchen table. She was wearing that old faded t-shirt I loved. "We'll have people in from all over who are probably confused about the saving message just like you were."

"No doubt," I agreed.

"I wonder if there's a way we could use our wedding to help them," she said.

"Ohh, yeah. Good idea," I said, now reveling in the rare moment of inclusion in the planning process. "I've got it!" With a dramatic tone, I leaned in and asked, "What do you want the first thing we do as a married couple to be?" She smiled deviously. "No, not that. I mean, the *very first thing.*"

"Oh, yeah!" she sang with delight, following my train of thought. We both cooed from the joyful impatience of the burgeoning idea. Though the plan for fabrics, and cake, and venue shifted multiple times before the day came, this secret plan was one aspect we both clung to, telling no one except Russ, the minister.

Now that the day had arrived, I was nervous. What we were going to do was unconventional. I'd never seen anyone do it, though I knew if there is one day a man can get away with saying almost anything he likes, it is the day he is the groom.

"I now pronounce you man and wife," Russ said. The audience clapped, not quite expecting what came next. "Kristah and Lucas have something they want to share with you." He handed the mic to me, and I turned to the audience.

"My wife and I," I said, throwing a sideways glance

at Kristah. The excitement of the word *wife* was like electricity on the tongue. "We have imagined all of the marvelous things we will do together once we're married. Though we wanted to start right, we want the very first thing we do as a married couple to be sharing the Gospel with those we love. Since I have a microphone and a *very* captive audience, that's what I'm going to do right now.

"For years, I thought that salvation was a free gift, but somehow also requires good works. Is eternal life free, or is it costly? The quest for that answer drove me deep into a barren wilderness. I wandered dryly in the desert following the footmarks of those who went before. I suffered isolation in the wild, but I clung to the path etched in the dry ground. I wanted an answer. I longed to rest. At the moment when I was ready to give up, a fellow traveler arrived and pointed to the distant horizon. I protested weakly, holding to the mysterious footprints I followed. She showed me that the complicated patterns in the sand were nothing more than my own tracks layered upon each other. I had been walking circles. I would never find what I was looking for on that path. God used Kristah to lead me out of the wilderness into this beautiful oasis I've named clarity. What I've come to see is simple. Salvation is as easy as believing and as free as a spring of living water in the desert.

"'For God so loved the world that he gave His only

begotten Son that whoever believes in Him will not perish but have eternal life.' It's as simple as that. Believe in Jesus for His promise of eternal life, and you have it. Believing in Him means that you're convinced that his promise is true. Eternal life is life with Him that you can never lose. If you believe in Him for that gift, then you have eternal life the moment you believe. Please don't leave here without believing in Him to receive eternal life."

I looked across the audience of family and friends. People stood around who I loved and admired. Nearly all the people I had ever loved, experienced loss, and been confused with were gazing back at me at that moment. Some of them had contributed to my confusion; some were the ones who helped bring me out. Would they understand what I just said? Only time would tell. I didn't want to linger too long within that moment, but I hoped that we had planted a seed. Finally, I raised the mic. "Now, let's party!" I said as I handed the microphone back to Russ.

As we walked down the flower-covered aisle, he said, "It's my pleasure to present Mr. and Mrs. Lucas Kitchen."

THE WAY WE CHANGE

The Gospel of grace often gets accused by naysayers, of being a license to sin. In my experience, it was salvation apart from works, sometimes called free grace, that gave me the foundation I needed to begin to mount a serious fight against my sin. Eventually, I had to call on my wife to help me with my porn habit. It had not magically disappeared as I thought it would once we got married. By God's grace and my wife's help, I quit using porn a number of years into our marriage.

Wanting to do something more meaningful than make a living, I quit my media business and joined the ministry which my father-in-law started and with which my wife was already working. It's called Free Grace International. Working with the ministry has allowed me to write a bunch of books about grace through faith. If you've ever struggled with the confusion that I have, I hope you'll consider taking a look at the books that my team and I have produced. They are specifically designed to help you get clarity on the subject.

As part of the ministry, I've also made hundreds of gospel related videos. We distribute these bite-size messages online. Last time I checked, we had a few million people who we've reached with the message of Christ through our media. You can connect with us on social media, youtube, or subscribe to one of our various websites, lucaskitchen.com, freegrace.in, lucasanswers.com.

I have also partnered with the Grace Evangelical Society. I speak at their regional and national conferences, and I'm one of the voices on their syndicated radio show. They distribute some of my books, and they have been a great source of inspiration and hope. You can find out about their ministry at faithalone.org.

My wife and I have two children now. Eli and Eily are little funnier and cuter versions of us. They remind us of all that is worth fighting for in the world. They not only keep us laughing, but they keep us praying. Nightly I talk to them about God's grace and the incredible gift of eternal life.

I suppose I should mention that I went back to seminary, a different seminary this time. I graduated recently. I'm now pastoring.

About once a year, Kristah and I   curl up on the couch to watch The Twilight Saga. Much of it we laugh at now, but that is part of the charm. It reminds us of who we were and who we are becoming as we head toward our eternal home. We still fight about who is the number one Twilight fan.

Printed in Great Britain
by Amazon